COMMUNIST EASTERN EUROPE

THE WALKER SUMMIT LIBRARY No. 2

COMMUNIST
EASTERN
EUROPE

Joseph Rothschild
Columbia University

WALKER AND COMPANY • NEW YORK

This study is concerned only with the so-called People's Democracies—Poland, Czechoslovakia, Hungary, Rumania, Bulgaria and Albania. The Communist states of Yugoslavia and East Germany are beyond its purview.

Published simultaneously in Canada by George J. McLeod, Limited, Toronto.

Library of Congress Catalog Card Number: 64-16805

Manufactured in the United States of America

iv

TABLE OF CONTENTS

Part I: Interpretation

Part II: Reference

v

From the End of
the First World War
to the End of the Second

CHAPTER ONE

The states of East Central Europe—Poland, Czechoslovakia, Hungary, Yugoslavia, Rumania, Bulgaria, Albania, Greece—were created, or restored, or enlarged, or truncated at the end of the First World War as a result of the concurrent and unexpected collapse toward the end of that war of the four great empires—Russian, German, Austro-Hungarian and Ottoman—which had for decades and centuries past dominated the East Central European area. High hopes accompanied the formation of the smaller, new, so-called "successor states." It was believed that their establishment met an imperative of justice by giving due (if only partial) recognition to the principle of nationalism, and it was expected that they would make a major contribution to the peace and stability of Europe.

These hopes ultimately proved abortive as they rested on an illusion of nonexistent strength in the post-Versailles East Central European area. The mere existence of the new states could not and did not prevent the revival of German and Russian military and economic power in the 1930's nor could it prevent these two giants flanking East Central Europe on the west and east from resuming their traditional policy of collaborating with each other at the expense of the lands between them. Despite post-1918 differences in ideologies and political structures, Germany and Russia were to pursue this policy throughout most of the period between the two world wars until its culmination in the Hitler-Stalin Pact of August 23, 1939, which provided for the partition of East Central Europe into respective Nazi German and Soviet Russian spheres of influence and conquest. As for the other great powers, who might be presumed to have had an interest in underwriting the East Central European states against the aggressive aspirations of Germany and Russia, the United States was remote and isolationist during the interwar decades, and Great Britain's European policy was based on the fallacious impression that France had emerged too powerful from the First World War and must be balanced by a revived Germany which should therefore be supported and appeased by Britain. London was, furthermore, myopically indifferent to the fate of East Central Europe as is graphically illustrated by Prime Minister Neville Chamberlain's remark during the September 1938 Munich crisis that the pivotal Czech-German confrontation was, after all, but ". . . a quarrel in a far-away country between people of whom we know nothing. . . ." Thirteen years earlier, in 1925, his half-brother, Foreign Minister Sir Austen Chamberlain, had expressed the same disastrous indifference with the private comment that "for the Polish

Corridor, no British government ever will or ever can risk the bones of a British grenadier." By the time this British aloofness was finally punctured in 1939, the sands had run out in independent East Central Europe. France, finally, by the 1930's was too weak —militarily, politically, economically, and psychologically—to sustain alone the Versailles settlement against Germany and Russia.

Quite apart from the malevolence or abdication of the great powers, the fragility of the interwar East Central European settlement was compounded by mutual rivalries and internal weaknesses among and within the successor states themselves. Poland and Czechoslovakia quarreled over territory (Teschen) and policy. Hungary aspired to regain her lost areas of Slovakia and Ruthenia from Czechoslovakia, of Transylvania from Rumania, and of the Voivodina (and possibly Croatia) from Yugoslavia. Bulgaria, Greece, and Yugoslavia, in turn, brawled over the disposition of Macedonia and Thrace.

Though nationalism had allegedly been the primary principle in drawing the postwar East Central European frontiers, large and disaffected ethnic minorities were assigned to most of the successor states: Germans, Jews, Ukrainians, and White Russians to Poland; Germans and Hungarians to Czechoslovakia (where, furthermore, there was considerable friction between Czechs and Slovaks themselves); Hungarians, Jews, Tartars, and Ukrainians to Rumania. Macedonians were a source of terror and violence in both Bulgaria and Yugoslavia, while in the latter country the hostility between Croats (Roman Catholic) and Serbs (Greek Orthodox) was even more debilitating than the Czech-Slovak discord to the north.

Economically, each of the successor states—with the possible exception of Czechoslovakia—suffered from an unfortunate rural-urban balance, shortage of capital and industry, rural overpopulation, underemployment, underconsumption, and low productivity. Western capital, in general, shunned massive investment in an area of such weakness and so obviously threatened by Germany and Russia. The relative poverty of the area and its economic vulnerability vis-à-vis "industrial" Europe were maximized by the world depression of the late 1920's and 1930's which stampeded the East Central European states (again, with the exception of Czechoslovakia) into abandoning the parliamentary political structures with which they had experimented during the "Versailles decade" of the 1920's (when the prestige of the seemingly invincible institutions of France seemed to require emulation by her East Central European protégés), in favor of royal or military or political dictatorships in the 1930's (when Germany and Italy appeared to be the most plausible models for imitation).

These dictatorships, however, and the swollen bureaucracies which sustained them, were brittle, ineffective, and irresolute despite their rhetorical bombast of "the strong hand." They lacked mass appeal and real ideological strength, were incapable of generating adequate economic development or military effectiveness, and were too pettily chauvinistic to cooperate in the defense of the area against external threats.

4

As a result of the combination of diplomatic, economic, political, and military impotence, the states of East Central Europe all succumbed to Nazi Germany's imperialist expansionism in the late 1930's and early 1940's. Bulgaria, Hungary, and Rumania became voluntary satellites of the Axis Powers; Czechoslovakia a relatively passive victim; Greece, Poland, and Yugoslavia resisting victims.

Nazi Germany, in her turn, had several policy options open to her in the area. She could continue a traditional "Prussian" preference for dividing East Central Europe with a friendly Russia, as epitomized in the Hitler-Stalin Pact, or she could switch to an "Austrian" policy of contesting the area with an estranged Russia, the choice for which Hitler finally opted with his initially successful attack on the Soviet Union on June 22, 1941. Once having ejected Russia from the entire area, Nazi Germany had a second set of choices open to her: the rational-functional one of developing the area or the ideological-racist one of despoiling, exploiting, and applying genocide to it in the alleged interest of German "folkish destiny." By deciding on the latter policy of violence and extermination (most ferociously toward Gypsies and Jews, but also to an appalling degree toward Poles, Russians, and Yugoslavs), the Nazi regime both damaged the German war effort and provoked that general moral revulsion against itself which was to fire Germany's foes and steel their determination to hammer her into the defeat of 1945.

Stalinist Stakes and Policies
After the Second World War

CHAPTER TWO

The fate of East Central Europe after the Second
World War was largely determined by the fact that
the major part of the area was liberated from German
power and occupation by Soviet, not Western, armies.
Only Greece, where the British army appeared first,
and Yugoslavia and Albania, largely self-liberated by
Partisan forces generously supported by Great Britain and the United States, were exceptions to this
rule of direct Soviet control. Yet the Yugoslav exception was not to appear politically consequential until
1948, or the Albanian until 1960, for the respective
leaderships of Marshal Tito and Enver Hoxha are fervently Communist and were initially passionately
pro-Soviet.

The Soviet Union, having been devastated during
the war, naturally and plausibly insisted that East
Central Europe must never again be permitted, or
permit itself, to become the staging area for an invasion of the Soviet Union. Hence Soviet security required that only regimes friendly to herself be in

power in the East Central European countries. So far the Western statesmen were prepared to agree. Yet Soviet ideology required a syllogistic construction which the West regarded as unwarranted but could not prevent the Soviet government, whose armies were in occupation of the area, from enforcing. The Kremlin, in short, insisted that only Communist regimes could be relied on to prove dependably friendly.

The Soviet stake in imposing Communist power upon East Central Europe was compounded of several rationales, expectations, and fears. For one thing, the replacement of "bourgeois" governments by Communist ones could be interpreted as both "demonstrating" the asserted superiority and "proving" the claimed historical inevitability of "socialism" as a system. On the other hand any attempt to reverse this process and oust the Communist regimes could and would be denounced as impermissible, politically reactionary, and historically retrogressive. Furthermore, the imposition of Communist rule in the area served as an expression of Russian national expansionism. As a strategic factor, East Central Europe could henceforth serve as a reverse staging area for a possible assault from the Soviet Union upon Central and Western Europe. Not only would East Central Europe be denied forever to German aggression, which had made such a searing impact upon the Soviet Union during 1941-45, but the Soviet Union would herself acquire a veto on German unification because her politico-military frontier would henceforth run through the heart of Europe. From the economic point of view, finally, a Communist-ruled East Central Europe could serve as an object of Soviet exploitation through such devices as: (1) "joint" Soviet-local companies, which were in fact managed to the exclusive advantage of the Soviet partner; (2) inequitable pricing arrangements under which the Soviet Union overcharged for the commodities that it sold to the East Central European countries and underpriced those that it bought from them, which, furthermore, were frequently resold by the Soviet Union to hard-currency non-Communist countries at enormous profits; and (3) during the initial postwar years, plain looting. Even though these raw Stalinist techniques of extortion have been modified or abandoned, Communist East Central Europe still remains economically useful to the Soviet Union as a spearhead for her politico-economic drive to infiltrate and influence the developing countries of Africa, Asia, and Latin America.

An exasperating and unsolved problem accrued, however, to the Soviet Union by virtue of the fact that her very drive to maximize her advantages and realize her stakes in East Central Europe created its own liabilities and elicited its very nemesis. The subjected peoples bitterly resented the destruction of the non-Communist political parties as well as the subversion of free and potentially democratic political and legal institutions. National dignity and pride were outraged by Soviet arrogance, contempt, and exploitation, a feeling even shared by some local Communist leaders. The Communist parties, furthermore, were flooded with waves of careerists, opportunists, and sadists who rushed to climb aboard the seemingly invincible bandwagons, thereby further diluting the parties' appeal and moral stature. Finally, the iron-fisted Soviet policy in East Central Europe undermined the positions and strengths of the Western European Communist parties. The strong and seemingly promising drives to power by the Communists of France and Italy were halted and reversed by the late 1940's. It is doubtful that Stalin was excessively troubled over this reversal of Communist fortunes in the West as he was throughout his life largely indifferent to the fate of Communist movements beyond the area of direct Soviet control. Even within his own sphere, however, his insistence on Soviet primacy led to the politically serious rift with Tito's Yugoslavia in 1948, as well as to embarrassing opposition on the part of a number of other nationally conscious Communist leaders in other East Central European countries who had to be purged to secure absolute and implicit compliance with Soviet demands and interests. It is therefore appropriate, at this point, to interrupt our general survey with a country-by-country examination of the process by which Communist power was imposed upon the states of East Central Europe and they were transformed into "People's Democracies."

Poland

CHAPTER THREE

In implementation of the Hitler-Stalin Pact, which provided for the partition of Poland, German armies invaded that country from the west on September 1 and Soviet armies struck from the east on September 17, 1939. Despite the fact that the Polish Government—which continued to function in exile first from Paris, then from London—reserved its claims to the entire pre-September territory of Poland, both Germany and the Soviet Union annexed considerable areas of prewar Poland. The Soviet share of the spoils amounted to slightly more than half the territory and approximately one third of the population of Poland. The people incorporated into the Soviet Union were mainly Jews, Ukrainians, and White Russians, with ethnic Poles but a minority — though a sizeable one — among them. The bulk of this territory had not been assigned to Poland by the Versailles powers in 1919, who regarded Russia's right to it as legitimate. Instead it had been conquered by Polish arms in 1920 at the time of revolutionary Russia's post-World War and Civil War exhaustion. Yet the Soviet government's decision to reassert its claims in mid-September 1939, while Poland was locked in mortal combat with Nazi Germany, was viewed by Poles as a stab in the back.

Though Poland and the Soviet Union became formal allies after Hitler's attack upon the Soviet Union on June 22, 1941, though the Polish Premier, General Wladyslaw Sikorski, paid a seemingly harmonious visit to Stalin in Moscow in December 1941, though the Soviet government agreed to the raising of a Polish army on Soviet soil*, nevertheless the territorial issue remained a source of friction since the Soviets adamantly refused to consider surrender of their post-September 1939 acquisitions while the Poles vehemently insisted on the integrity of their prewar frontiers. After the battle of Stalingrad in the winter of 1942-1943, the Soviet hand was immensely strengthened. Thus, when the Polish government in London requested an International Red Cross investigation of the massacre of several thousand Polish officers whose corpses were discovered in April 1943 in the Katyn Forest, the Soviet government used the occasion to break off diplomatic relations with its troublesome Polish ally. The Poles, by refusing to blame the Germans (who had discovered the mass graves) and calling instead for a neutral investigation, appeared to imply (as was probably the case) that the officers, who had been serving in Soviet-occupied Polish terri-

---

*Commanded by General Wladyslaw Anders and transferred in 1942 to the British-controlled Middle East and subsequently to the Italian war theater.

tory in September 1939, had been murdered by Soviet authorities.

Relations with the exile Polish government having thus been broken, the Soviet government proceeded to create its own, Communist-dominated, rival Polish government (the "Lublin Committee") which it unveiled and installed in July 1944 shortly after the Soviet armies had advanced westward into Polish territory which the Soviet Union did not claim as its own. With the Soviet armies there also served a Communist-officered Polish corps, commanded by General Zygmunt Berling. This had been raised, beginning in February 1943, after the departure from the Soviet Union of the inimical Anders army and had first seen action on October 10, 1943. To eliminate the major remaining source of opposition, the Soviets callously permitted the Germans to decimate the underground Polish Home Army which was loyal to the exile government in London, by failing to assist the ill-fated Warsaw Uprising of August 1 – October 3, 1944. Later, during their own advance across Poland and into Germany, the Soviets liquidated the remnants of this anti-German and anti-Communist Home Army. Thus, at the conclusion of the war, Soviet and Communist power in Poland was paramount and, as events were to show, not seriously compromised by Stalin's agreement at the Yalta Conference in February 1945 to a "broadening" of the Soviet-sponsored "Lublin Government" by the cooptation of a handful of "London" Poles, headed by Peasant Party leader Stanislaw Mikolajczyk. The latter had succeeded to the premiership of the London exile government upon the death of General Sikorski in an airplane crash at Gibraltar on July 4, 1943.

Soviet policy in Poland, however, involved more than mere repression. To advance Soviet power into the heart of Central Europe and to impell Polish nationalists to look henceforth to Soviet Russia for protection, Stalin compensated Poland for the loss of her prewar eastern territories by the transfer to the postwar state of extensive western acquisitions up to the Oder-Neisse Line as well as in southern East Prussia. This area was carved out of prewar Germany, from which the German population was now expelled, to be replaced by Polish colonists. Since Poland's wartime losses at the hands of Nazi Germany totaled six million dead, half of whom were Polish Jews, and since there had been physical destruction on a vast scale, this acquisition of formerly German territory was and is viewed with satisfaction by virtually all strata of Poles. It remains the main tie of identity between the public and the regime and perhaps the only popular bond between Poland and her Soviet patron.

Comparing Poland's eastern losses and western gains, the latter appear to outweigh the former in every way except area. The 70,000 square miles lost to the Soviet Union contained oil, gas, and potassium deposits, much forest land but also extensive swamps. The 39,000 square miles acquired from Germany gave Poland a 300-mile coast-line with the valuable Baltic ports of Gdansk (Danzig) and Szczecin (Stettin), the Silesian industrial complex with its rich coal, zinc, lead, electrical, metallurgical, and engineering industries, and 15 million acres of relatively fertile farm land. Thus, although Poland's postwar area is but 120,000 square miles as compared to the prewar 150,000, the balance between industry and agriculture is sounder, the capacity of both these sectors of the economy greater, her frontier with Germany more defensible (283 miles as contrasted with 1,188 in 1939), and her population ethnically and confessionally more homogeneous due to the extermination of Jews and the loss to Russia of the largely White Russian and Ukrainian-populated eastern territories. However, although these changes appear to many to be an accomplished fact, it should be noted that the United States has officially recognized only the Soviet acquisitions from Poland but not the Polish ones from Germany. Hence Poland remains diplomatically dependent on the Soviet Union as the one Great Power committed and able to support her against any possible German claims.

The "broadening" of the Communist-dominated "Lublin" government by the inclusion of a minority of "London" Poles did not loosen the Communist grip on Poland nor was it really a genuine concession. In 1945 the Communists had neither the personnel nor the capacity to run the Polish state. Economists, technicians, administrators—many living in exile—were required and could be lured back to Poland only through participation in the government of the "Londoners." Their presence in Warsaw also minimized the danger of widespread civil war between the government and surviving elements of the Home Army whose remaining nests were not finally destroyed until 1948.

Communist political strategy during the immediate postwar years envisaged three goals. First it aimed to isolate and decapitate Mikolajczyk's Peasant Party, which represented the vast anti-Communist majority of the nation. Then it successfully sought to destroy the Socialists by infiltration and by forcing them to fuse with the Communist Party on the latter's terms. Finally, the Communist Party itself was to be purged of those who, animated by some degree of national pride, were not prepared to subordinate all Polish interests to Soviet ones.

The achievement of the first object of this line of action was facilitated by political blunders on Mikolajczyk's part. In a national referendum on June 30, 1946, he confused his supporters by insisting that they vote to retain a Senate despite the fact that in prewar days the Peasant Party had favored the abolition of an upper house. He even purged his own party of five other leaders who opposed his tactics on this issue. Mikolajczyk had decided that it was essential to differentiate his own Peasant Party from the Socialists and Communists and rashly chose the Senate issue as a means since on all other questions at stake in the crucial referendum of June 30, including the acquisition of the western territories, land distribution, industrialization, and limited nationalization, it was both morally and politically impossible to oppose the proposals jointly endorsed by every other major party.

As a result the Communists were able to encourage the splitting off from the Peasant Party of splinter groups which were dissatisfied with Mikolajczyk's leadership and at the same time to prevent the Socialists from coming to an understanding with him by judiciously exploiting some dubious incidents and disreputable people hiding under the respectable cloak of Mikolajczyk. Indeed, Poland remained a restless land in 1946. Home Army guerrillas, Ukrainian (Bandera) bands, police terror, and student demonstrations all kept the country in turmoil. In the southern town of Kielce, 39 Jews were killed and 40 wounded in a pogrom on July 5. In the circumstances, the logic of his tactics was forcing Mikolajczyk into increasingly negative opposition while police repression and vigorous Communist action kept him on the defensive and isolated. In the parliamentary elections of January 19, 1947, which followed a campaign characterized by extensive intimidation, Mikolajczyk's party received only 27 seats and 1,154,847 votes. The Government Bloc which comprised Communists, Socialists, dissident Peasants, and a spurious "Democratic" Party, polled 9,003,682 ballots and gained 392 seats while 25 seats went to several pseudo-independent parties with 1,086,344 popular votes.*

Mikolajczyk, his usefulness to the Communists now at an end, was dropped from the cabinet in which he had been Deputy Premier and Minister of Agriculture. Soon, even personal opposition outside the government became untenable as the split between East and West was intensified after announcement of the Marshall Plan. As the chief opponent of the

---

*All ballot statistics given here are official ones and have been challenged as fraudulent.

Communists, Mikolajczyk fled Poland in October 1947. By May 1948, it was possible to fuse the remnants of his once-powerful party with two splinter groups to form a United Peasant Party which became a docile member of a Communist-dominated coalition.

With the threat of an independent Peasant Movement eliminated, the Communists maximized their pressure on the Socialists. The prewar Polish Socialist Party (PPS) had participated in the London exile government as well as in the underground Home Army loyal to it. In 1942, however, a rival Polish Socialist Workers Party (RPPS) was founded in German-occupied Cracow which soon established cordial relations with the underground Communist Party (PPR) and eventually became a major participant in the Soviet-sponsored "Lublin Committee." At war's end the restoration of the old, regular PPS was prohibited and those of its militants who served in the Home Army were hunted down. Thus, PPS veterans had little choice but to join the RPPS, thereby, however, providing the latter party with a mass base, diluting its dependence on the Communists, and committing it to contacts with Western Socialist parties. For a time it appeared that Communist tactics had backfired. The RPPS, now feeling its oats, proceeded to win a series of trade-union and works-council elections from the Communists, to demand a greater role in the cabinet, to deny the Communist claim to be the "leading party" in the government coalition, and in general to behave with alarming independence. In August and again in November 1946, its leaders,

Edward Osobka-Morawski, Stanislaw Szwalbe, and Jozef Cyrankiewicz, were summoned to Moscow together with Communist leaders Wladyslaw Gomulka, Jakob Berman, and Roman Zambrowski in a forceful Soviet attempt to end their public rivalry. At the second of these meetings the RPPS was compelled to accept collaboration with the Communists for the January 19, 1947, parliamentary elections in return for a promise that its organizational independence and separate identity would be respected.

It is hardly surprising that until the defeat of Mikolajczyk's Peasant Party in these elections of early 1947 the Communists treated the RPPS with caution. They could not move against it openly lest it desert its Communist ally and join forces with the Peasants. Though there was some sentiment within the RPPS for such a change of partners, it never came about, as the RPPS leaders feared to provoke outright Soviet intervention and as they came to the conclusion that too many reactionaries had found a home in the Peasants Party. Once the elections were over, however, and Mikolajczyk out of the government, the Communists lost no time in going back on the promise made in Moscow in November 1946. They demanded that the RPPS end its independent existence and that it fuse into the Communist Party. There was prolonged and courageous resistance to this ominous demand which necessitated yet another summons to Moscow in January 1948 and a Party purge in September. Nevertheless increasing isolation and the force of Russian pressure bludgeoned the RPPS into submission. The formal fusion congress took place in Warsaw in December 1948 and eight of the eleven members of the Politburo of the resultant Polish United Workers Party (PZPR) were Communists, thus giving the latter unquestioned dominance. Nevertheless, it is a fact that some ex-Socialists always remained in the top leadership of the merged party and were, indeed, to play crucial roles in the "October Days" of 1956.

The major sources of opposition to Communist rule in Poland had now been effectively eliminated. Yet the job of securing total submission to the dictates of the Soviet Union, which was Stalin's paramount goal during his last years, was not yet fully accomplished. Therein lies the irony of the fact that the most vehement and even savage Communist voice to demand the political suicide of the independent RPPS had been that of the Communist Secretary-General, Wladyslaw Gomulka. Hardly had he achieved his end when he himself became the most prominent victim of an internal purge among the Communists.

While most of the prominent Polish Communist leaders had spent the war years in the Soviet Union, Wladyslaw Gomulka had been active in the anti-German Communist underground movement in Poland, of which he became the head in November 1943. After the war he was Secretary-General of the Communist Party, a Deputy Premier, and Minister for the Re-Acquired Territories, in charge of the former German lands now incorporated into Poland. He was seemingly all-powerful. Gomulka's only apparent weakness was the weakness of the entire Polish Communist Party. It had not organized the nation's major anti-German resistance movement as, for instance, had the Yugoslav Communists. It had no genuine mass popularity such as the Czechoslovak Communists enjoyed. It did not operate in a political environment where other parties had compromised themselves by collaboration with the Germans as, for instance, in Hungary. It was all too closely identified with Russia, one of the nation's two historic foes, was numerically weak partly because of the Stalinist purges of the 1930's, and was internally divided between war-time "Muscovites" and "undergrounders." Acutely conscious of these deficiencies, Gomulka wished to bolster his Party by identifying it with national goals and aspirations. This required avoiding mass terror, not alienating the peasantry through premature collectivization, emulating the mass appeal and nationalism of the prewar Socialist movement, and finding a distinctive "Polish road to Socialism."

In the spring and summer of 1948, however, Titoist Yugoslavia successfully asserted her political independence through resistance to Soviet pressures. Stalin's reaction to this unprecedented development was to institute a ruthless purge of all Communist leaders in East Central Europe whom he suspected of placing "local," national interests ahead of Soviet priorities. Gomulka was an obvious culprit and hence victim. He accepted the allegations of Polish nationalism but with admirable and stubborn courage refused to concede his positions to be erroneous. As a result, his popularity in the country and among the Communist rank-and-file rose so sharply that the "Muscovite" majority of the Politburo was forced to negotiate and plead with him rather than being able to resort to arbitrary measures. Nevertheless, he was deprived of his State and Party offices one by one and was finally arrested in July 1951, after the imprisonment of several lesser "nationalist" Communists who, like himself, had been in the underground rather than in Soviet sanctuary. Yet his reputation as the one Communist leader who had attempted to defend Polish interests while the others were all too willing to sacrifice them was such that the "Muscovites" dared not execute him as was the lot of similar leaders in other East European countries.

As a final expression of contempt for and hatred of Polish nationalism, Stalin in November 1949—the month in which Gomulka was expelled from the Central Committee—imposed Soviet Marshal Konstantin Rokossovsky upon Poland as Minister of Defense, Commander-in-Chief of the Armed Forces, and, after May 1950, Politburo member. Significantly, it was Rokossovsky who had commanded the Soviet armies which, in the late summer of 1944, had remained immobile while the Germans crushed the Warsaw Uprising.

An all-out industrialization drive and accelerated collectivization campaign next ensued. The latter totally failed to improve or to rationalize Polish agriculture while the former overemphasized heavy industry and, with the outbreak of the Korean War in June 1950, the manufacture of armaments. It also required heavy sacrifices in consumption and housing, and involved inordinate waste, lack of coordination, and neglect of quality. This program was so blatantly geared to Soviet rather than Polish national interests that the Polish people, though viewing the goal of industrialization as desirable in principle, were driven to sullen resentment by the manner of its application in practice, a resentment maximized by the concomitant increase in terror and repression which reached an apogee in the early 1950's. After Stalin's death on March 5, 1953, and particularly after Nikita Khrushchev's denunciation of Stalin's crimes at the Twentieth Congress of the Soviet Communist Party on February 24-25, 1956, the Polish "Muscovite" Communist leadership began to lose its grip and its self-confidence. The public, as well as the national Communist leaders, were quick to sense this, took courage, and extracted the liberalization measures of 1956, which will be discussed more fully later on.

Czechoslovakia

CHAPTER FOUR

Czechoslovakia under Nazi occupation was relatively docile and prosperous. True, the assassination of Hitler's Deputy-Protector Reinhard Heydrich who was mortally wounded May 27 and died June 4, 1942, did elicit a savage reprisal which resulted in the notorious annihilation of the town of Lidice. Also, from August to November 1944 an abortive insurrection, with nationalist and Communist participation, was launched in Slovakia. In general, however, Czechoslovakia suffered substantially less human and material damage during the war than did Poland. German repression was directed largely against the intelligentsia and the Jews rather than the nation at large. Thanks to Allied bombings of Germany, much industry was actually moved into Czech lands while the peasants also maintained a marked prosperity. Russia being for many Czechoslovaks a traditional patron, rather than an historic foe, relations between the Czechoslovak exile government in London and the Soviet Union were far more cordial than those enjoyed by its Polish counterpart. Indeed, while the latter was denied both Soviet recognition and permission to return to Warsaw, the Czechoslovak government, led by President Edward Benes, returned to Prague in May 1945 with Soviet approval. The cordial relations which Benes had established with Stalin during an earlier pilgrimage in December 1943 appeared to be confirmed in Moscow during the homeward journey. The Czechoslovak surrender of the eastern-most province of Ruthenia to the Soviet Union in January 1945 proceeded relatively smoothly. Ruthenia was in any event poor and inhabited by a Ukrainian-speaking population. Its possession by the Soviet Union is primarily of politico-strategic importance; not only does it eliminate the possibility of an anti-Soviet Ukrainian "Piedmont" but also it gives the Soviet army direct access over the Carpathian mountain passes to the Hungarian plain—an advantage which was to be demonstrated later when the Hungarian revolt of November 1956 was crushed by Russian troops.

The Communists were strongly represented in the government with which Benes returned to Czechoslovakia and held some powerful cards vis-à-vis their political rivals and the President himself. They were not identified with the Munich surrender (1938). They could and did garner prestige from the war performance of the Soviet army and could likewise cultivate the historic Russophilism of the Czechoslovak nation. They had been a major and a legal party in prewar Czechoslovakia. They now capitalized on an intensified Slovak nationalism and under a Communist Minister of the Interior turned to their own advantage the turmoil, patriotic fervor, and patronage opportunities created by the wholesale expulsion of the German and, to a lesser extent, the Hungarian minorities. The Communists also enjoyed solid, though not exclusive, support from a working class alienated from "bourgeois society" less by economic misery than by rigid social barriers.

These advantages encouraged the Czechoslovak Communist leaders, among whom the most prominent were Klement Gottwald and Rudolf Slansky, to attempt an electoral conquest of power rather than an illegal seizure of it. This initial reticence to stage a *coup* suited and may even have been dictated by Stalin's diplomacy in the immediate postwar years. Many Western liberals and Socialists then regarded traditionally democratic Czechoslovakia as a test case of Soviet intentions in Central Europe while Stalin did not yet care to embarrass the Belgian, French, and Italian Communist parties during a period when their participation in coalition governments seemed useful.

Taking their chances on achieving an electoral victory, the Czechoslovak Communists permitted the parliamentary elections of May 26, 1946, to proceed without interference and emerged as the largest single party with 38 per cent of the popular vote. Though impressive, this was something of a Pyrrhic victory as the other parties concluded that this point marked the crest of the Communist tide. They became bolder in exposing and prosecuting Communist abuses and intimidation. New members enrolled *en masse* in the Czech (National) Socialist and Catholic Populist parties. Public opinion polls confirmed that Communist popularity was ebbing. In November 1947, the Social Democrats, who had polled 13 per cent in the May 1946 election, replaced their fellow-traveling chairman Zdenek Fierlinger with a leader less amenable to Communist manipulation. Thus arose the Communists' fear that their "Marxist majority" with the Social Democrats comprising their own 38 per cent plus the latter's 13 per cent of voting strength was jeopardized. Communist hopes of winning an absolute majority alone were also dimmed. Since the Cold War had already frozen in 1947 due largely to Soviet conduct elsewhere in Eastern Europe, and Communist participation in the Western European governments had ceased, there were now no longer any paramount international reasons for Czechoslovak Communists to hesitate to seize power before it eluded them altogether. Accordingly they staged the notorious *coup* of February 1948, unwittingly aided by their opponents who foolishly chose to resign from the cabinet as a showdown protest against Communist tactics in the government. President Benes knuckled under to Communist pressure as he had at Munich in 1938 to that of Germany. Fierlinger, with Communist aid, resumed his leadership of the Social Democrats. Simultaneously the Soviet Union, through its special emissary Valerian Zorin, gave far firmer support to the Communists than their foes received from the West.

The result of the crisis was rapid and ominous. On March 10, 1948, occurred the violent death of the non-partisan Foreign Minister Jan Masaryk, son of the founder and first president of Czechoslovakia. On April 18, the pliant Fierlinger merged his rump Social Democratic Party with the Communists. On April 29, all industrial plants employing more than 50 workers were nationalized.* On May 9, a cowed parliament by a vote of 246 to 0, with 54 deputies either in flight or prison, adopted a new, Communist-tailored constitution. On June 7, Benes resigned the Presidency in favor of the Communist leader Gottwald rather than put his own signature to the new document. Characteristically, Benes had prepared two letters of presidential resignation—a tough one, protesting the undemocratic features of the new constitution, and an innocuous one which he eventually chose to sign. In the autumn, the judicial system and security administration were toughened and politicized.

The Czechoslovak Communists thus came to power in 1948 under conditions far more favorable than those which had confronted the Russian Bolsheviks in 1917 or the Polish Communists after 1944. With three years (1945-1948) of governmental experience behind them they now inherited a smoothly functioning state apparatus which they needed neither to smash (as Lenin had found necessary) nor to rebuild from wartime ruins (as the Polish Communists had been obliged to do after 1944) but could harness to their own purposes.

Czechoslovakia already being highly industrialized, and considerable land redistribution and nationalization having taken place before their *coup*,

---

*In October 1945, a presidential decree had nationalized all factories employing over 400 workers.

the Communists found their socio-economic task after 1948 easier than did their Polish comrades. The main imperatives were to expand heavy industry at the expense of light, to reorient foreign trade from the traditional Western markets and sources of supply toward the Soviet bloc, and to launch the collectivization of agriculture. All this was to be undertaken with great energy and drive in a series of five-year plans the first of which was announced on October 7, 1948, and launched on January 1, 1949.

Some drawbacks, however, marred this vista. The February 1948 *coup* aroused widespread bitterness and the Communists' obvious dependence on Soviet support and shameless readiness to place Soviet over Czechoslovak interests elicited contempt. In the course of several recruitment drives between 1945 and 1948 the Communist Party had ceased to be an elite and had opened its gates to a flood of opportunists and careerists.* These had now to be screened and purged, a process which tended to be frustrated by nepotism and cliqueism. Nor was it easy to replenish the ranks with people whom the Communist Party wanted the most. Workers, technicians, and scientists knew that the regime needed them anyhow and thus chose to remain aloof rather than subject themselves to the risks and boredoms of active Party membership. Government bureaucrats and office-seekers desiring promotion and anxious to guarantee themselves against undesirable job transfers thus remained the principal aspirants to membership.

*By 1953 members from prewar days were only 1.5 per cent of the total membership.

In the event, not only has the Communist Party failed to keep itself sociologically proletarian, it also finds difficulty in recruiting young people and collectivized farmers. Slovaks, too, have remained underrepresented thanks to the persistence of a strong religious tradition, greater depredations by the Red Army during 1944-45, and Communist hostility to Slovak national aspirations after 1948.

More immediate and drastic in its impact was the political crisis which resulted from Tito's defiance of Stalin and the Cominform. In Czechoslovakia, as in Poland, Stalin responded by forcing the elimination of Communist leaders whom he suspected of not being fully committed to Soviet primacy and interests. The Czechoslovak purge was, however, more ferocious and more complicated than that of Gomulka and his "nationalist," "undergrounder" veterans. Its overtones were decidedly anti-Semitic and its victims ran through a puzzlingly wide political spectrum from Foreign Minister Vladimir Clementis—a moderate, "Slovak nationalist" who, though a Communist, had passed his wartime exile in London rather than in Moscow—to Secretary-General Rudolf Slansky, a Jew and "Muscovite," who had been flown from the Soviet Union into Slovakia during the anti-Axis uprising of 1944. The purge began with Clementis' removal from his post on March 14, 1950, reached its apogee with the hanging of Clementis, Slansky, and nine other victims on December 3, 1952, and apparently closed with long prison sentences meted out to lesser culprits in January 1954. In sharp contrast to the example of other Communist regimes and the Soviet Union itself, the Czechoslovak leaders long and stubbornly refused to engage in a post-Stalinist rehabilitation of these purge victims. In its formal organizational pattern as well as its political style, the Czechoslovak Communist Party imitates the Soviet one. Its "line" and policy have, however, in recent years been more Stalinist than its mentor's. "Free and businesslike discussion" is a myth and "fearless criticism," though rhetorically demanded, has largely remained a manipulative device. The Czechoslovak Communist leaders, at whose head currently stands Antonin Novotny, apparently have considered their roots among the masses to be so shallow as to permit only a pale imitation of the post-Stalinist thaw and relaxation. For some time, in fact, they even jammed the "fraternal" Polish radio to protect their subjects from contamination by Gomulka's "national Communist" ideas. In reality, however, they have apparently had little to fear from domestic "revisionist" pressures, perhaps because the execution of Clementis eliminated the likeliest "national Communist" leader. In recent years, Novotny has been able to resist an attempt led by Rudolf Barak, who was Interior Minister until June 1961 and Deputy Premier and Politburo member until his expulsion and arrest in February 1962, publicly to reopen the Clementis-Slansky case. Barak, however, was relatively popular within the Communist Party and may well be heard from again in the future especially since there is much recent evidence to suggest that while there may not yet be an easy alternative to Novotny's leadership, dissatisfaction and unrest within the Czechoslovak Party and intelligentsia are now beginning to be expressed with increasing persistence.

As regards economic and institutional developments, "socialism" appears to be well established in Czechoslovakia notwithstanding some recent setbacks. As of January 1961, 88 per cent of the arable land was reportedly collectivized while four-fifths of the remaining 12 per cent consisted of dwarf holdings of less than 12 acres. In 1960, 96 per cent of the national income was derived from the "socialist," state-owned and cooperative, sector of the economy. Czechoslovak industry and its products in fact make a major contribution to the Soviet drive for politico-economic influence over developing nations. So much so perhaps that the Czechoslovak public resents the extensive exports to poorer countries and blames them for domestic consumer-goods shortages.

The roots of the difficulty, however, are clearly deeper as shown by the fact that the Czechoslavak economy, which was long viewed as the most efficient in the entire Communist bloc, has recently faltered most seriously. The third five-year plan (1961-1965) had to be abandoned in July 1962 despite the fact that its production targets had not originally appeared to be extraordinarily ambitious. Agriculture and heavy engineering were the branches which failed most blatantly, and many construction projects remained unfinished. Productivity, national income, investment, and foreign trade were all under their targets while inventories rose uneconomically due to dislocations resulting from sudden planning changes and to low transportation capacity. Many planning errors appear to have been made which are not likely to be remedied easily or quickly. Too many different machinery items have been produced instead of specializing in a few and thus achieving economies of scale. There has been excessive concentration on import-intensive industries such as machine tools for which heavy ore imports are required. Traditional export industries including glass, ceramics, and shoes have been neglected. In 1963, therefore, the sobered planning authorities decided to funnel the bulk of their investments into agriculture, transportation, fuel, and power while expecting only a modest one per cent increase in industrial output.

In the political sphere, July 11, 1960, witnessed the adoption of a new constitution which formalizes the power monopoly of the Communist Party and officially proclaims Czechoslovakia to be a "Socialist State" and "part of the world socialist system." This constitution is markedly more centrist than that of 1948, a fact which appears to have aroused uneasiness among the Slovaks, to whom the regime has been obliged to give assurances that less regional autonomy will, on the other hand, facilitate the economic development of Slovakia which has hitherto lagged behind the richer Czech lands.

Unlike most of the other Communist-ruled countries, which have collective heads of state, Czechoslovakia, under its new constitution, retains the individualized Presidency, whose current incumbent is Antonin Novotny. This appears to be an attempt to capitalize on the nation's historical attachment to the occupant of the Prague castle, the Hradcany—seat of the old kings of Bohemia and of the Founder-President Thomas Masaryk.

A moderate cultural ferment is in progress in Czechoslovakia with Western plays dominating the stage and Greenwich Village-type clubs catering to a youth hungry for jazz and the "theatre of the absurd." This trend has not been welcomed by the nervous authorities who sought to limit such Western influences by installing in 1962 Europe's first known television-jamming station, which seeks to blanket with visual snow the "subversive" programs originating in Vienna.

The attempt to win political influence in the developing nations by educating their students in Czechoslovakia has not been an unqualified success as many of the African scholarship students resent the Communist ideological indoctrination, police surveillance, and cool public reception which they have experienced. A more serious domestic political problem looms ahead as a result of an upsurge during 1963 of Slovak nationalism, which manifests itself as anti-Czech and anti-centralistic sentiments within the Slovak Communist Party. This development appears to be connected with the pressures to rehabilitate fully the victims of the Clementis-Slansky purges of the Stalin era and thus represents an implied threat to President Antonin Novotny, the major surviving beneficiary of those purges.*

---

*In August 1963 the purge victims were legally but not politically rehabilitated, i.e., they were cleared of the charges in the original indictment but not exonerated from their alleged "crimes against the Party."

Hungary

CHAPTER FIVE

Hungary, unlike Poland and Czechoslovakia, was, during the Second World War, not a victim but a partner of Nazi Germany. Through this alliance she briefly recovered some of her historic territories lost in 1919, including southern Slovakia, Ruthenia, northern Transylvania, and western Voivodina. In order to press her claim to the rest of Transylvania at Rumania's expense, Hungary participated in the German invasion of the Soviet Union where her army was eventually cut to pieces at Voronezh in January 1943. Somewhat earlier an allied but rival Rumanian army had been shattered in the Soviet counterattack at Stalingrad in November 1942. Thus one of the grimmer ironies of the war was presented in the spectacle of Hungary and Rumania competing for Hitler's favor so as to achieve territorial gains at one another's expense.

Following the withdrawal of the remnants of her army from Russia in April 1943, Hungary made cautious but unavailing attempts to leave the war.

German forces occupied the country in March 1944 and ruled it through pliant premiers despite the increasing disenchantment of the long-time Regent and Chief of State, Admiral Miklos Horthy, who was eventually deported to Germany in October 1944. During the winter of 1944-1945, Hungary became a war theater as the German army made one of its last defensive stands along the Danube River against advancing Russian forces. Looting and the fighting during the siege of Budapest which lasted from December 24, 1944, to February 13, 1945, were both immensely destructive.

In December 1944, the Soviets established in that part of Hungary which they then controlled a provisional government with strong Communist participation. As in Czechoslovakia, the Hungarian Communists were initially moderate, worked with great zeal to rebuild the devastated country, and directed their main political efforts to preventing their Socialist, Smallholder, and National Peasant coalition partners from falling under vigorously anti-Communist leadership. They also worked hard to prevent the numerically weak Communists from being squeezed out of the coalition government of the liberated country. When, nevertheless, on October 7, 1945, the Communists sustained a severe defeat in the Budapest municipal elections, the Soviet occupation authorities on their behalf pressured all other parties into agreeing to preserve a coalition government no matter what the results of later parliamentary elections might be. When these were held on November 4, 1945, the Smallholders received 59 per cent of the vote, the Socialists and Communists 17 per cent each, and the National Peasants 5 per cent. The Smallholders were thus prevented by their earlier pledge from forming the one-party cabinet to which their electoral strength clearly entitled them. They even had to accede to a Communist demand for the crucial Interior Ministry portfolio which was first assigned to the Moscow-oriented but moderate Communist Imre Nagy and in March 1946 transferred to the tougher "underground" Communist Laszlo Rajk who had spent the last years of the war in Horthy-ite internment.

In 1946, the Communists launched a persistent and eventually successful campaign to break the Smallholder Party. Repeatedly it was forced to purge itself of real or alleged fascist sympathizers, and its leaders were blackmailed for their previous connections with Horthy as well as for private reasons. The Communists also held out the false hope that compliance with their wishes would win Soviet backing for the return of Transylvania by Rumania to Hungary. At the same time Soviet occupation authorities lent a hand to the local Party by arresting particularly stiff-necked Smallholder leaders, usually on charges of pro-Nazi collaboration. By the summer of 1947, the Smallholder Party was a fairly pliant instrument of Communist manipulation; Hungary bowed to Soviet pressure in declining participation in the Marshall Plan; and the parliamentary elections of August 31—though not yet thoroughly totalitarian —were sufficiently unfree to result in a disastrous decline in Smallholder strength from 59 per cent in

1945 to 14 per cent of the vote. The Communists emerged as the largest party albeit with only 22 per cent while the Socialists and National Peasants received 15 per cent and 9 per cent respectively, and an agglomeration of opposition parties totaled 35 per cent. The 5 per cent German minority was simply disenfranchised and the opposition parties, having served the function of dispersing the anti-Communist vote, were now systematically destroyed one by one over a year and a half period. Following a familiar pattern, the Socialists were forced to fuse with the Communists in June 1948. By May 15, 1949, the Communists were at last ready to stage their first really totalitarian elections in which the Government list of candidates received 95.6 per cent of the votes. This was followed by the promulgation on August 20, 1949, of a new Communist constitution under which Hungary officially became a "People's Democracy."

The Communists and the Soviet occupation authorities had, however, psychologically overplayed their hand. Their conduct was so brutal as to be counter-productive. It killed whatever frail buds of genuine friendship for the Soviet Union may have flowered during the initial postwar period of Communist moderation. Even the workers, aware of Soviet exploitation, angered over the emasculation of the trade unions, sullen about their low real incomes, first turned apathetic and then hostile. With the destruction of the other political parties, the Roman Catholic Church became for a while the chief institutional obstacle to total Communist domination. Its effective political resistance was, however, smashed with the arrest and public trial first of the conservative Primate, Jozsef Cardinal Mindszenty, who was arrested December 26, 1948, and sentenced to life imprisonment on February 8, 1949, and then of Archbishop Jozsef Grosz, arrested in May 1951 and sentenced to fifteen years' imprisonment on June 28. The Calvinist and Jewish ecclesiastical organizations were also repressed though their political problems were rendered somewhat easier by the fact that their superior religious dignitaries were not appointed from abroad.

Culture and education were now Sovietized (the cult of Stalin reaching more ludicrous proportions in Hungary than anywhere else within the Soviet orbit). This may well explain why the youth of the country was, in the end, so completely alienated as to become a kind of bridge which came to link the latent opposition of workers, peasants, and intellectuals.

On the economic front, outright Soviet looting in the immediate postwar years (by July 1947, Soviet requisitions, reparations, and occupation costs had come to absorb about 35 per cent of the national income) later gave way to more sophisticated techniques of exploitation. Key sectors of the economy were, until November 1954, assigned to special joint Hungarian-Soviet companies, the management of which was dominated by the Soviets. All real and alleged former German assets as well as Hungary's uranium mines were sequestered outright by the USSR. Nationalization proceeded step by step until, by a decree of December 28, 1949, only enterprises employing less than ten workers remained in the private sector of the economy. An insanely high investment rate built a spectacular but irrationally overdeveloped heavy industrial complex for which Hungary lacked the needed raw materials while labor productivity and living standards declined. In agriculture, too, over-hasty and overly ambitious collectivization drives, characterized by mismanagement, inadequate and defective capital equipment, and peasant sabotage, reduced the average annual grain production during the 1950-1954 five-year plan to levels below those of 1911-1915. The resulting chaos and the near-mutinous temper of the workers and peasants led the regime to introduce the ameliorative "New Course" in July 1953. Under the relatively popular leadership of Communist veteran Imre Nagy the pace of economic growth was slowed, some improvements in living standards was instituted, and the political terror which had so far characterized Communist rule was markedly relaxed.

Nagy had been one of the victims of the purge which Stalin had inflicted on the Hungarian as well as the other East Central European Communist parties in the wake of Tito's defection. Having, however, spent the war years in the Soviet Union, Nagy apparently had sufficiently powerful friends among the Soviet leaders—perhaps including Georgi Malenkov—to escape execution. Less fortunate was the more radical "native" Communist Laszlo Rajk, who had succeeded Nagy as Interior Minister in March 1946 and was executed on October 15, 1949, after a singularly repellent "show trial" which found him and several co-defendants guilty of Titoism, treason, and other alleged crimes. The man who climbed to power as Stalin's chief Hungarian satrap on the basis of these purges, the "Muscovite" Matyas Rakosi, then instituted the overly ambitious heavy-industrialization and agricultural-collectivization policies. It was because he was known to have originally opposed their introduction that Nagy was installed in the premiership on July 4, 1953, when their failure had become manifest. For the next three years a mortal personal and political struggle was waged between Imre Nagy as Premier and Rakosi, who retained the First Secretaryship of the Communist Party and hence control of its *apparat*, centering on the relative merits of moderate as against tough economic and political policies. Their duel, and the vacillating Soviet attitude toward it, finally kindled the Hungarian Revolt of October-November 1956, to be discussed in a later chapter.

Rumania

CHAPTER SIX

The Rumanian army which participated in the German invasion of the Soviet Union in order to reconquer Bessarabia and persuade Hitler to recognize Rumania's claim to northern Transylvania was severely mauled at Stalingrad during the winter of 1942-1943 and shared in Germany's subsequent reverses. Later, as the Soviet armies approached the Rumanian frontier, King Michael staged a royal *coup d'état* against his pro-German government on August 23, 1944, and opened the front to the advancing Soviet army. Two days later, on August 25, he declared war on Germany. With this decisive action, King Michael opened all of southeastern Europe to the Soviet advance and, as events were to show, won Allied support for Rumania's recovery of the whole of Transylvania.

As long as Rumania was in the war theater, her new government was one in which the military predominated. Not until the beginning of 1945 did the Communist Party bid for power and, supported by tough Soviet pressure on King Michael, achieve the appointment on March 6, 1945, of a Communist-dominated Cabinet. Coming close upon the heels of the

Yalta Conference (February 4-12, 1945) this arbitrary Communist-Soviet intervention was angrily denounced by the United States. Washington, in fact, declined to recognize this new government which was formally led by the pro-Communist stooge Petru Groza. This episode may properly be seen as the first move in the Cold War.

American persistence at the Potsdam Conference of July 17 to August 2, 1945, in refusing recognition to Groza's Communist-dominated government encouraged King Michael to attempt to rid himself of it. But as Groza had Soviet support and as the Soviet, not the American, army was stationed in Rumania, King Michael could do no better than withdraw to his summer palace and refuse to sign decrees, which did little to alter the existing situation. Finally, at the Moscow Conference of Foreign Ministers on December 16-27, 1945, the United States reversed its stand and agreed to recognition on the understanding that representatives from the anti-Communist Liberal and National Peasant parties would be included in the cabinet and that free parliamentary elections would be held eventually. Since, however, American and British recognition on February 4, 1946, preceded the elections held on November 19, 1946, the Americans and British had deprived themselves of effective leverage to insure their free character while the two anti-Communists co-opted into the cabinet on January 7, 1946, were simply ignored.

These elections of November 19, 1946, were preceded and accompanied by such a crass campaign of intimidation, falsification, manipulation, discrimination, and murder that the victory of the Communist-controlled Government Bloc was a foregone conclusion. In the spring of 1947, there followed a wave of arrests of opposition politicians, the most prominent of whom were tried and sentenced in November on charges of criminal conspiracy with American "imperialism." Simultaneously the Communists removed from the cabinet the less reliable although docile among their coalition partners and concluded their assumption of total political power by forcing the abdication of King Michael on December 30, 1947, followed by the proclamation of a republic. The finishing touch was provided when in February 1948 the Communists absorbed the Socialist Party, already purged of its anti-Communist members in March 1946.

On March 28, 1948, totalitarian-style elections returned an overwhelmingly Communist National Assembly which on April 13, 1948, ratified a "People's Republican" constitution. One interesting feature of this constitution was its attempt to come to grips with minority problems. A considerable degree of administrative autonomy was given to the Hungarian minority of Transylvania. A later constitution, ratified on September 24, 1952, expanded this experiment in ethnic pacification by conceding to the Hungarian minority its own Autonomous Region, modeled on the Soviet constitution of 1936, and granting cultural but not regional autonomy to the Armenian, Bulgarian, German, Greek, Gypsy, Tartar, Turkish, and Ukrainian minorities. Two ethnic minorities, however, continued to suffer from discrimination: the Jews and the Yugoslavs, both of whom were suspected of loyalty to foreign, and allegedly hostile, states. The definition of Yugoslavia as hostile was, of course, an outgrowth of the Stalin-Tito controversy which in Rumania, as in other Soviet satellites, elicited a series of internal Communist purges. When the dust from these had settled, it developed that the victims were either "nationalist," "undergrounder" Communists, as in the case of Lucretiu Patrascanu, or "Muscovites" of ethnic minority stock, as for instance Emil Bodnaras (Ukrainian), Vasile Luca (Magyar-Szekler), and Ana Pauker (Jewish). The outstanding victor, Gheorghe Gheorghiu-Dej, was both "Muscovite" and ethnically Rumanian. Policy differences probably also divided victors and victims. There is reason to suspect that Patrascanu, who had been Justice Minister, was offended by the brutal tactics of his colleagues, their heavy-handed violation of national sensitivities, and their subservience to even the most outrageous Soviet demands. Luca, in turn, as Finance Minister, appears to have been skeptical about the overly ambitious industrialization and collectivization drives which were launched in the aftermath of the Tito crisis very much as they were in all the other satellites.

Rumania's economic recovery from war destruction and voracious postwar Soviet reparations exactions was rather slow. In 1946, agricultural production was only 59 per cent of the 1934-1938 average while industrial production was at best but 77 per cent of what it had been in 1941. This disap-

44

pointing performance supplied the rationale for a vehement attack on all forms of private property in 1948. A series of nationalizations, currency reforms, collectivization drives, and economic plans (one one-year plan, two five-year plans, one six-year plan) were launched, beginning with 1948-1949. The industrial achievements resulting from these measures, though impressive on a comparative basis, remained so far below the planned goals because of low productivity, high costs, absenteeism, embezzlement, and slowdowns, that the regime, probably frightened by the November 1956 revolt in neighboring Hungary, revised its industrial goals downward and its wage scale upward in December 1956. As a New Year's gift to the peasants, compulsory agricultural deliveries were abandoned on January 1, 1957, but poor rural leadership, faulty agricultural price structures, inadequate mechanization, and peasant recalcitrance continue to keep agricultural productivity so low that Rumania, once one of Europe's chief granaries, has become a grain importer. By February 1961, 48 per cent of the peasant population had been collectivized while the proportion of land in the "socialist sector" had reached 72.7 per cent of the arable land by the spring of 1960. In fact, however, much of the so-called "socialist sector" in agriculture consists of unions of individual peasants retaining title to their own land.

In cultural matters, the Communist authorities have consistently, but vainly, sought to "Russify" and proletarianize the consciousness and tastes of the Rumanian people, who appear nevertheless to have remained incorrigibly "French" and bourgeois. The churches have been emasculated as potential strongholds of opposition, with the Orthodox hierarchy purged into docility during 1947-1948 and the Uniate Church forcibly reabsorbed into the Orthodox between October and December 1948. (The same fate also befell the Uniate churches in the other People's Democracies and the Soviet Union, since their affiliation with the Vatican made them politically suspect to these regimes.) With the religious institutions thus effectively silenced and "synchronized," the fount of moral and political resistance to totalitarianization has been the intelligentsia, with the University of Cluj in Transylvania seemingly the headquarters of recent cultural ferment.

Though perhaps less well known than the Polish Rapacki Plan of October 2, 1957, for the neutralization of Central Europe, Rumania advanced her own Stoica Plan on September 16, 1957. Its purpose was to propose disengagement in the Balkans, and though Greece and Turkey rejected this overture, Rumania has continued to hope for some form of eventual agreement by unilaterally reducing her own armed forces by 20 per cent in 1958. For the past several years she has also quietly permitted the resumption of emigration to Israel, having apparently become convinced that the Rumanian Jews are obdurately unabsorbable into a "proletarian" culture.

Though it has been uneven in recent years, Rumania's economic development has shown some interesting features. As in all the other states of the Soviet orbit, agricultural production has suffered recurrent reverses, most notably so in 1962. On the other hand, industrial production has risen more rapidly in Rumania than in any of the other bloc countries. Between 1960 and 1962 it increased by 55 per cent or 15.8 per cent annually, a rate which was not substantially slowed during 1963.

Much of the credit for this impressive record must be ascribed to the petro-chemical industry as well as to a broader upsurge of labor productivity. Rumania, too, has shown a marked degree of independence in developing its pattern of foreign trade. Commercial ties with the West have been increasing rapidly since 1962 when the first British industrial fair was held in Bucharest, and there has been consistent interest in broadening trade and technical assistance contacts with such major Asian countries as India and Indonesia. And while the volume of trade between Rumania and other Communist countries has, of course, been growing as well, it is particularly noteworthy that Rumanian officials have been stubborn and apparently successful in resisting pressures from the Council for Mutual Economic Assistance (CEMA) which might tend to relegate their country to the position of a raw-material producer and manufacturer of oil-drilling and refinery equipment. They have, instead, been insistent on maintaining a more balanced pattern of industrial advance and have displayed a degree of self-assertion which has even found echoes in the political and ideological sphere, where Rumania, perhaps more than any other East European country, has maintained a detached attitude toward the mounting Sino-Soviet dispute.

Bulgaria

CHAPTER SEVEN

Bulgaria, like Hungary and Rumania, was allied with the Axis Powers during the Second World War but, unlike them, did not declare war on the Soviet Union or make her army available to Hitler for his eastern campaign. She rendered economic aid and supplied Black Sea naval facilities to Germany but her major war aim was limited to the incorporation into Bulgaria of the Macedonian areas of Greece and Yugoslavia (as well as Greek Thrace) which she regarded as her own by ethnic, geographical, and historical right. Between 1941 and 1944 this aim was temporarily achieved, but Bulgaria failed in her efforts to withdraw from her German alliance. After Rumania's switch of allegiance in August 1944, Bulgaria's dilemma became acute and she promptly sought peace with the Western Allies and the royal Greek and Yugoslav governments-in-exile. Since Bulgaria was never at war with the Soviet Union, she was technically entitled to establish direct contact with her actual enemies. What was legally justifiable was not, however, politically wise. Bulgaria might have done better to request mediation by the Soviet legation in Sofia. The Soviet government, as events showed, immediately became suspicious of direct Bulgarian-Western contacts which might cheat Moscow of that "temporary military control" of Bulgaria which the Western Allies had conceded to her in a secret agreement of June 1944. The result was that the USSR declared war on Bulgaria on September 5 which was followed by an unopposed Soviet invasion even though no German troops were garrisoned in Bulgaria. On September 9, a *coup d'état*, aided by the treachery of the War Minister and rendered successful by Soviet intervention, ousted the Bulgarian government and installed the so-called Fatherland Front, a wartime clandestine coalition composed of Communists, the left-wing Peasant Union, some Socialists, intellectuals, army officers, and soon also the small Radical Party. Thus the Fatherland Front was composed of all Bulgarian political forces which considered the attempt to realize the nation's territorial aspirations on the basis of Axis affiliation as so misguided as to warrant outright subversion. It had indulged in some wartime sabotage and raised some guerrilla forces which were, however, insignificant compared with Tito's Partisans in Yugoslavia or the Polish Home Army.

The Fatherland Front government installed by the *coup* of September 9, 1944, made the Bulgarian army available to the Soviet command which utilized it in the remaining stages of the war. This army gave a good account of itself, suffering over 30,000 casualties, and thereby impressing the Allies sufficiently to elicit relatively light peace terms. The areas of Macedonia and Thrace seized during the war had to be restored to Yugoslavia and Greece, but Bulgaria was permitted to retain the Southern Dobruja, acquired in 1940 at Rumania's expense. Bulgaria's $25 million reparations debt to Yugoslavia was canceled by Tito during the immediate postwar heyday of intra-Communist solidarity and friendship. The Soviet Union, in contrast with her policy toward Germany, Hungary, and Rumania, demanded no reparations. War damage was less than that suffered by any other East Central European country.

Although the Communist Party was numerically small in 1944, it possessed a viable and nationwide organization, enjoyed some prestige by virtue of its twenty-year underground struggle against a series of semi-competent or quasi-dictatorial governments, and benefited from the impressive successes of the Soviet army. The major advantage enjoyed by the Communists in their subsequent drive to total power was not, however, local strength but rather the backing of the Soviet Union.

In the first Fatherland Front cabinet of sixteen, the Communists were assigned four portfolios, including those of the Interior, which controlled the police, and of Justice. Under the pretext of purging pro-Germans and fascist collaborators, the Communists then manipulated these ministries to advance their party interests and settle many an old political and personal score. Indeed, the Bulgarian purge of real and alleged Nazi sympathizers was perhaps the severest of any in the East Central European countries, resulting in thousands of executions even though the nation's involvement with the Axis Powers was the most marginal of all. Particularly ominous was the fact that even those ministers who had sought to take Bulgaria out of the war in early September 1944 were imprisoned. Their offense, presumably, was that they were pro-Western rather than pro-Soviet. In any event, the severity of the purge aroused both shock and indignation from which the Peasant Union member of the Fatherland Front initially seemed to benefit most directly.

In September 1944, the leader of the Peasant Union, Dr. G. M. Dimitrov, who had fled the country in 1941, returned from Cairo but declined to join the Fatherland Front cabinet, preferring instead to devote himself to the job of rebuilding the Peasant Union of which he was Secretary-General. With the opening of hostilities between Communists and British forces in Greece in December 1944, the Bulgarian Communists and their Soviet backers appear to have come to the conclusion that the pro-Western G. M. Dimitrov was too dangerous to be permitted a powerful role and consequently launched a campaign of vilification against him, specifically charging him with being a British agent and of spreading defeatism among the Bulgarian troops then fighting with the Soviet army against the Germans. Forced to resign the Secretary-Generalship of the Peasant Union in January 1945, and placed under house arrest, G. M. Dimitrov escaped abroad in August after seeking refuge with the American representative in Bulgaria. His successor, Nikola Petkov, who had spent the war years in Bulgaria as a Fatherland Front leader, also found himself unable to work with the

Communists. He resigned the Secretary-Generalship of the Peasant Union in May 1945 and quit the cabinet in August, at which time some of the leading Socialists also left it. Thus the "official" Fatherland Front-affiliated Peasant and Socialist parties fell into the hands of pro-Communist stooges. Yet the opposition wings of both parties, respectively led by Petkov and Kosta Lulchev, remained strong, and received impressive American and British backing. This circumstance obliged the Communists to cancel the rigged elections which had been prepared for August 28, 1945, evidently because they did not wish to antagonize the West before receiving diplomatic recognition and a peace treaty.

Some political concessions ensued which made possible organizational and propagandistic activities by the opposition. Unfortunately, however, early Anglo-American support encouraged Petkov and Lulchev to overplay their hand. They proclaimed their refusal to participate in any future elections unless the Communists surrendered control of the Interior and Justice ministries. The proposed elections were nevertheless held on November 18, 1945, after the return of the veteran Communist hero Georgi Dimitrov, who had lived for more than a decade in the Soviet Union. The electoral campaign having been far from free, both the United States and Britain renewed their protests concerning the Bulgarian situation at the Moscow Foreign Ministers Conference in December 1945, with the result that the powers agreed to broaden the Bulgarian government by the inclusion of two members of the opposition, much as was done in Rumania. When, however, Soviet Deputy Foreign Minister Andrej Vyshinsky arrived in Sofia in January 1946 to implement this agreement he found, to his consternation and irritation, that Petkov and Lulchev were both standing firm on their earlier demand for control of the Interior and Justice ministries. The Bulgarian opposition was evidently not prepared to be intimidated as easily as its Rumanian counterpart. By March 1946, indeed, the Bulgarian Communists themselves had retreated to the point of agreeing that the opposition should receive the Justice portfolio and nominate two undersecretaries in the Interior Ministry, a plan which did not go into effect only because the Soviet authorities vetoed it after deciding to push for complete Sovietization of Bulgaria regardless of its impact on the West.

The first blow of the renewed Communist offensive fell on the army. On July 2, 1946, control over it was transferred from General Damyan Velchev, a non-Communist member of the Fatherland Front, to the cabinet as a whole. About 2,000 "reactionary" officers were dismissed. Velchev was obliged to resign the War Ministry to the veteran Communist Georgi Damyanov in September 1946, to become Bulgarian minister to Switzerland, where he died in 1954.

A plebiscite held on September 8, 1946, determined by a majority of 92.32 per cent that the Bulgarian kingdom should be replaced by a republic. The subsequent October 27, 1946, elections for a constituent assembly saw the opposition, led with reckless courage by Petkov, win 22 per cent of the votes despite intimidation and terror. In a free election, claimed Petkov, he would have been supported by 60 per cent of the electorate. The Communists were now merely waiting for the American ratification of the Bulgarian Peace Treaty before eliminating the opposition, and when this occurred on June 4, 1947, Petkov was promptly arrested on the floor of the legislature on the following day. Tried in August amid a hysterical anti-American campaign and condemned to death, he was hanged on September 23, 1947. On August 26, his independent Peasant Union had been dissolved, leaving only the Communist-controlled Fatherland Front Peasant Union in existence. The turn of the opposition Socialists came a year later with the arrest and imprisonment of Lulchev and several colleagues in 1948. The destruction of his independent Socialist Party was accompanied by the forced merger of the Fatherland Front Socialists with the Communist Party in August 1948. Early in 1949 the Radical Party and the intellectuals' *Zveno* group dissolved themselves, leaving in existence only the Communist and purged Peasant parties. The latter is simply the docile rural arm of the former while the Fatherland Front has become a mass organization, incorporating 40 per cent of the population, whose program is that of the Communist Party. By the end of 1948, therefore, Communist political control of Bulgaria was absolute and the administrative, economic, and cultural transformation of the country could begin.

As elsewhere in the bloc, the inevitable internal crisis produced by the Stalin-Tito rift wracked the

Bulgarian Communist Party. The victims of the ensuing purge were the "native," and "nationalist," Communists, led by Traicho Kostov who was executed on December 16, 1949, after a sensational trial in the course of which he repudiated his pretrial confession to political crimes, a confession which had been wrung from him under torture. The victors, again, were the "Muscovites" among whom the most Stalinist was Valko Chervenkov, who became the Soviet satrap of Bulgaria upon the deaths of the veterans Georgi Dimitrov (July 2, 1949) and Vasil Kolarov (January 23, 1950).

The Communists' economic program for Bulgaria has been institutionalized in one two-year plan (1947-1948) and four consecutive five-year economic plans (1949-1965) which have cumulatively resulted in the well-nigh total collectivization of agriculture and nationalization of industry and commerce but which have not achieved the planned production goals in many sectors of the economy. Indeed, the economic failures have been such that several leading Communists were removed from office in 1957 and again in 1961. Unofficial food rationing was introduced in September 1961, and inflationary pressures forced a currency revaluation on January 1, 1962.

Despite some concessions in the post-Stalin years to meet the most critical consumer needs, heavy industry has remained the prime investment sector of the regime. Since nature appears to have endowed Bulgaria rather poorly both with iron ore and coal deposits, the wisdom of developing heavy industry seems dubious. It duplicates at great expense, and therefore wastefully, the facilities available in Bulgaria's Communist sister states. Reliance on a greater division of labor and national specialization within the bloc, together with concentration of investment on Bulgaria's traditional economic resources in agriculture and light industry, would have been more rational. Yet, somewhat as in the Rumanian case, Bulgaria has steadily resisted the suggestion that she become little more than a vegetable and tobacco supplier to the bloc.

Following the Soviet example, Bulgaria permitted some political relaxation after Stalin's death. Many of her Communist leaders are, however, reluctant to follow Khrushchev's policy of reconciliation with Tito, as the Macedonian irredentist issue is as sore a wound for them as it was for pre-Communist Bulgarian governments. Intellectuals have been particularly vehement in demanding political liberalization while peasant stubbornness has exerted steady economic pressure on the regime. After a series of political ups and downs, the Stalinist Valko Chervenkov was himself definitely purged from the premiership in 1962. Traicho Kostov was posthumously rehabilitated in 1956 as a gesture to Bulgarian nationalism and to Marshal Tito. Most recently the leadership of Communist Bulgaria has devolved upon Todor Zhivkov, who, though a "native" Party veteran, appears to enjoy the implicit confidence of Nikita Khrushchev.

Despite this change of leadership, however, Bulgaria's economic development during 1962-1963 continued to emphasize industry at the expense of agriculture and consumer goods. Indeed, a number of commodities such as bread, salt, canned goods, sugar, ready-made clothes, and textiles, were in consistently short supply due to distribution and production failures. Lack of fodder resulted in excessive poultry and livestock slaughter with resultant shortages of eggs and dairy products. Drought wreaked havoc on the 1962 cereal harvest. Despite these difficulties, the Zhivkov government has fixed its sights on ambitious horizons. The current five-year plan (1961-1965) has been subsumed within a twenty-year plan which foresees total production in 1980 as 2.5 times the levels of 1961. Top priority will continue to be given to producer goods, with a 400 per cent increase in coal and a twentyfold rise in pig-iron production expected. The discovery in late 1963 of apparently extensive petroleum and natural gas deposits has further whetted Bulgaria's industrial appetites.

In the area of foreign policy the most interesting recent development has been an improvement in relations with Yugoslavia as a result of which a modern road is to be built between Nish and Dimitrovgrad while technical, cultural, and commercial exchanges are to be facilitated and increased. The Bulgarians have also undertaken a major effort to woo the developing nations, a campaign which, however, suffered a damaging setback as a result of the devastating experiences suffered by African students who arrived in Bulgaria in substantial numbers during the early months of 1962 but largely withdrew toward the turn of the year as a result of repeated clashes with the Bulgarian students and authorities.

The Crisis Year of 1956

CHAPTER EIGHT

There has, so far, been no discussion here of Polish and Hungarian developments since the mid-1950's. It is therefore imperative to return to these two countries whose internal crises in 1956 shook the entire Communist world and created grave and lasting problems for Soviet authority in East Central Europe.

The Soviet decision to impose total and direct control over East Central Europe following Tito's successful defiance in 1948 not only outraged local nationalism but fatally undermined the prospect for future rational economic planning. In addition it also paralyzed the respective Communist parties of the area politically. Their ideological vitality petrified into sterile dogma; the dynamic mobilization of social power degenerated into static imitation of the Soviet example; policy on all levels was vulgarized into the rationalization of power. A vicious circle of terror servility, corruption, and isolation closed around the Communist parties.

With Stalin's death on March 5, 1953, and the resultant period of hesitation, vacillation, and experimentation on the part of his Soviet heirs, the Communist parties of East Central Europe, having long since ossified into robots, were thrown into confusion. Their self-confidence was suddenly shaken. Simultaneously, the peoples regained a measure of hope, vigor, and militancy from the cultural thaw, economic concessions, political relaxation, and abatement of police terror which preceded and followed Nikita Khrushchev's denunciation of Stalin's crimes at the Twentieth Congress of the Communist Party of the Soviet Union on February 24-25, 1956. This confluence of the disintegrative process within the elites and the fortified resolution of the masses reached its climax toward the end of 1956 in Poland and Hungary. Khrushchev's visit of reconciliation to Tito in the spring of 1955 was also a contributory factor as it seemed to legitimize nationalism in the Communist bloc and undermine the various Stalinist leaders who had climbed to power through the purges which followed Tito's break with Stalin in 1948.

The post-Stalinist liberalization in Poland began, not with economic concessions, but rather with the reassertion by the Communist Party of its political control over the secret police and with official demands for the observance of "socialist legality." There followed a cultural revolt by young people and writers against the stultifying imperatives of "socialist realism." Demanding adherence to sincerity and truth, they proceeded to organize unofficial discussion groups, such as the famous Warsaw Crooked

Circle, which provided Party and non-party intellectuals with a forum in which to discuss outstanding public issues and served as a point of contact between workers and intelligentsia. In the wake of Khrushchev's "secret" speech of February 1956, which denounced Stalin's crimes, the leading Polish Stalinists either died opportunely of natural causes, as in the case of Boleslaw Bierut, or were removed from office by way of concession to national feeling as happened with Politburo members Jakob Berman, Hilary Minc, and Stanislaw Radkiewicz. In the spring of 1956 the hated "yellow curtain" shops where the privileged could purchase commodities not available to the general public were abolished, thus forcing the Party elite to rub shoulders with the masses for the first time in many years. Pressure against the Roman Catholic Church was relaxed, the good name of the wartime Home Army was partially rehabilitated, some genuine debates in the Polish parliament were once again permitted, and 30,000 prisoners, of whom 9,000 were held for political offenses, received amnesties. Still, the Soviets were unwilling to permit the restoration to office or power of Wladyslaw Gomulka, the national Communist leader gradually purged between 1948 and 1951, who had been quietly released from prison in December 1954 though the fact was not publicly known until April 1956.

The leadership of the Polish Communist Party at this time showed remarkable political skill in containing the nation's political and economic resentments and guiding popular energies into a struggle for gradual change, thus avoiding the twin threats of mass insurrection and Soviet intervention. On June 28, 1956, however, the workers and citizens of the industrial city of Poznan rose in a revolt which was provoked by accumulated political and economic grievances and witnessed by many Western visitors attending an international trade fair which was in progress at the time. More than 50 people were killed and over 300 wounded before order could be restored. The moral shock which this uprising dealt the Communist Party was immense precisely because the industrial proletariat had sparked and led so spectacular a demonstration of non-confidence in the regime. At the subsequent inquest by a plenary session of the Party's Central Committee on July 18-28, 1956, the Polish leadership repudiated the Soviet assertion that the Poznan tragedy had been the work of "imperialist agents" and apologized instead to the working people for the "immense wrongs" inflicted on them. It also promised to correct past injustices, to raise living standards, and to reduce the oppressive weight of bureaucratization. Yet the basic political decisions leading to Gomulka's full return to power and the inauguration of his policy of a "national Polish road to Socialism" were postponed for fear of a Soviet crackdown. Gomulka's conditions for placing his great personal prestige at the service of the Party by returning to the post of First Secretary and thereby rescuing it from increasing national ferment were as follows: (1) the complete vindication of his stand during 1948-1951; (2) abandonment of the collectivization of agriculture as unproductive and excessively offensive to peasant sentiment; (3)

the pursuit of Polish national interests if necessary even over the objections of the Soviet Union; (4) the selection of a new Politburo to be composed of men in whom he could have confidence; (5) the exclusion of Soviet Marshal Rokossovsky from this Politburo.

Fear that Moscow would not accede to such a program was certainly plausible. On the other hand, the nation's feelings, symbolized in the pilgrimage of a million people to the national religious shrine of the Jasna Gora monastery at Czestochowa on August 26, 1956, could no longer be ignored. Some crucial preliminary decisions were taken during the late summer of 1956. The then First Secretary of the Polish Communist Party, Edward Ochab, traveled to China where he apparently received Mao Tse-Tung's support for Polish "national Communist" aspirations despite objections voiced by Soviet Deputy Premier Anastas Mikoyan, who was in Peking at the same time. Upon his return to Warsaw in mid-September, Ochab was thus inclined to lean toward Gomulka's position. Meanwhile, on August 24, 1956, while Rokossovsky, who also served as the Polish Defense Minister, was on vacation, Prime Minister Jozef Cyrankiewicz, a former RPPS Socialist leader, detached the Internal Security Corps of the armed forces from Rokossovsky's control and placed it under the command of General Waclaw Komar, a nationalist Pole who had been jailed during the heyday of Stalinism in the early 1950's.

By mid-October, Ochab and a majority of the Party's leadership had accepted Gomulka's conditions. Yet at this juncture the die-hard "Muscovite" faction of the Politburo attempted a *coup d'état* with the aid of Rokossovsky's military units which failed only because it was blocked by General Komar's detachments and met with the refusal of most Polish officers and troops to permit themselves to be used against the national cause. The workers of Warsaw also mobilized in support of the new Gomulka-Ochab-Cyrankiewicz coalition. Thereupon, on October 19, 1956, the most imposing of conceivable Soviet delegations flew into Warsaw to try to block the imminent return of Gomulka to a position of undisputed leadership. Comprising Premier Khrushchev himself, Mikoyan, Molotov, Kaganovich, Marshals Konev and Antonov, and about ten generals, the delegation's arrival in Warsaw was accompanied by ominous movements of Soviet troops in East Germany, the Soviet Union, and within Poland itself. The Poles, now solidly led by Gomulka, Ochab, and Cyrankiewicz, stood their ground and threatened to fight unless Soviet troop movements were halted and the Polish Party left free to determine its own leadership. Once assured that Gomulka had no intention of permitting political power to pass from the Communist Party or of withdrawing Poland from the Soviet bloc, Khrushchev and his colleagues backed down. Evidently, they were not prepared to risk an open clash between their army and the Polish forces. Though their mission had failed they returned to Moscow on October 20. The next day Gomulka was elected First Secretary of the Polish Communist Party and Rokossovsky dropped from its Politburo and shortly afterward from the post of Defense Minister.

Gomulka's problem now became that of proving that he could really stabilize the fluid Polish political situation at the point of "national Communism" and stem the drift toward a disintegration of Communist power and secession from the Soviet orbit. His ability to achieve this was the condition of continued Soviet abstention from armed intervention, the seriousness of which the Soviets amply demonstrated by their subsequent actions in Hungary. Given this situation, Gomulka faced the Polish people with the blunt truth that they would henceforth have more freedom to experiment within a Communist framework but none to experiment with another political system. On October 28, 1956, the Roman Catholic Primate, Stefan Cardinal Wyszynski, was released from the arrest to which he had been confined since September 26, 1953, and threw his weight into the scales on behalf of Gomulka who had already reconfirmed the reputation first earned in the dark years of 1948-1951 as the national hero ready to "defend Poland" against Russian domination and exactions. In the meantime, the Soviet annihilation of the Hungarian revolt provided the Polish nation with a somber warning of what it could expect if it were not content to accept "national Communism."

Since 1956, Gomulka's Poland has remained, despite some retreats from that year's apogee, the Communist state with the greatest degree of political freedom. The peasantry is permitted to hold 87 per cent of the cultivated area in private ownership. The nation continues either to reject or be indifferent to Communist ideology while still accepting Gomulka's government as a political necessity and a geographical imperative. Indeed, with the growing military power of a West Germany which refuses to accept the postwar Oder-Neisse frontier (as does the United States), the Polish nation has come to accept membership in the Communist bloc as a guarantee of territorial security. Within that bloc in which their country is the third largest state, the Poles feel themselves to be a substantial power which may well benefit from the current Sino-Soviet rift. At the same time Poland pursues her security interests vis-à-vis Germany vigorously by persistent sponsorship of proposals for disengagement and neutralization in Central Europe, not merely through such official schemes as the Rapacki Plan, but also indirectly through a gradual resumption of her traditional cultural ties with the West.

Recent developments in Poland have been characterized by relative pragmatism in economic matters and by periodic attempts at political control over cultural expression. An apparently chronic fodder shortage led the government to decide on a sharp increase of investments in agriculture during 1963. Gross production was up 8.5 per cent in 1962 over the previous year but agriculture lagged due to inadequate mechanization, a condition which more recent investment programs are designed to correct. Living standards have also been deteriorating.

In 1963, it was announced that, on an experimental basis, thirty-four factories producing for export would be exempted from the price, wage, and production-quota requirements of the central plan and would be permitted to operate under "free-market" conditions with an assured priority of access to necessary raw materials. Significantly, the influential weekly *Polityka*, whose editor is known to be close to Gomulka, has suggested the wider extension of this experiment.

On the cultural scene, however, there has been a marked retreat from the apogee of cultural freedom reached during 1957. The government's efforts, begun in 1958, to curb the activities of the intelligentsia have continued ever since. Comparatively speaking, these have been moderate, but they have not failed to meet with determined opposition from writers, artists, and university students and faculty who have continued to probe ways in which to expand the area of freedom in their country and to seek contacts with the Western world. Partly as a result of these internal pressures, cultural exchanges with Western Europe and America have continued to receive official sanction while the government has only acted with severity in cases where Communist institutions and policies have been the subject of overt criticism or satire. A case in point was the enforced closing of Warsaw's candid and courageous Crooked Circle discussion club in February 1962. Inevitably, this has produced a state of almost endemic friction between the authorities and the Polish intellectual community as it has, on another level, led to substantial friction between church and state. Here too, however, while the days of freedom and collaboration which characterized the Polish October and its immediate aftermath are a thing of the past, it does remain true that the Roman Catholic hierarchy is able to continue its work under comparatively fewer restraints than in any other Communist country. The accumulation of all these political, economic and morale problems has brought in its wake a considerable erosion of Gomulka's former popularity.

In this atmosphere of uneasy equilibrium between freedom and restraint it has proved very difficult for the authorities to rekindle the enthusiasm of several years ago, particularly among young people, whose disinterest in and apathy toward ideological issues is a source of official concern. This very fact, however, may explain in turn why Poland has been perhaps the most successful country in the bloc in wooing African and Asian students to its educational institutions and the one in which there have, so far, been no ugly racial incidents. Obliquely, it may also account for Poland's comparative success in broadening its economic relationships with the developing countries, in which area she has been a relative latecomer but highly respected for the calibre of her personnel and a breadth of view which is not always characteristic of other Communist emissaries.

Turning now to the 1956 crisis in Hungary, it will be seen immediately that it partly paralleled and tragically diverged from the Polish pattern.

Four months after Stalin's death, the relatively popular Imre Nagy, Hungary's would-be counterpart to Gomulka, was appointed Premier, on July 4, 1953, to restore at least some degree of confidence in the Communist regime and to bring a semblance of order to the economy which had virtually disintegrated under the pressure of Matyas Rakosi's preposterously overambitious and thoroughly "Stalinist" industrialization and collectivization drives after 1948. Though Nagy as Premier now shaped the Government's program, Rakosi remained First Secretary of the Party and thus continued to control actual sources of power in the state and the government. Nagy proceeded to end the virtually indiscriminate use of terror, to grant amnesties to thousands of political prisoners, and to rationalize the economy by easing exaggerated industrialization goals, draconian work discipline, and unproductive collectivization. This so-called "new course" was, however, bitterly opposed and partly sabotaged by Rakosi, who was finally able to settle scores with his rival when Nagy's chief Soviet protector, Georgi Malenkov, fell from power in February 1955. Thereupon, in March, the Rakosi-controlled Central Committee of the Hungarian Communist Party condemned Nagy's policy. In April it deposed him as Premier, and in November expelled him from the Party.

Though Rakosi was strong enough to oust Nagy and to resume "Stalinist" economic policies, he was forbidden by the Soviet leaders, who had committed themselves to practice "socialist legality," from restoring the terror which alone could produce the desired results. Thus after the revelation of Stalin's guilt by Khrushchev at the Twentieth Congress of the CPSU in February 1956, the Hungarian intellectuals demanded an inquest into Rakosi's own past crimes, the chief among which was the judicial murder in 1949 of his "national" Communist rival Laszlo

Rajk, whose innocence Rakosi had, in fact, to concede on March 28, 1956. Nor could Rakosi destroy the prestige of Nagy and the popularity of the "new course" as alternatives to himself and his policy. Thus trapped in a vicious circle, Rakosi sought to slash his way free by proposing, on July 12, 1956, the arrest of Nagy and 400 rebellious intellectuals. At this point the Soviet leaders intervened. Anastas Mikoyan was sent to Budapest and deposed Rakosi on July 18, 1956.

This Soviet action was, however, a half-measure since Rakosi was replaced, not by the popular Nagy, but by Erno Gero, a man too closely identified with Rakosi to inspire confidence. The nation, the intellectuals, the anti-Stalinist Communists had tasted blood with Rakosi's fall. Their appetite was merely whetted by the solemn reburial of Laszlo Rajk on October 6, when 300,000 people walked past the coffin in a mass gesture of moral indictment against the regime. They were aware of the Poznan uprising and had no reason to be satisfied by the restoration of Party membership (but without office or power) to Imre Nagy on October 13. They were finally galvanized into action by the news that in Poland the top Soviet leaders had been successfully defied with Gomulka's return to power.

On October 23, 1956, demands voiced at a mass demonstration of Budapest citizens for an expression of solidarity with Poland and for greater freedom in Hungary were brusquely rejected by the new Party chief Erno Gero. Simultaneously the secret police fired into the crowd. It was this brutal and ill-conceived act which led to spontaneous and armed resistance which spread rapidly into a nation-wide uprising. In contrast to the new Polish Communist leadership, which had stood firm against Soviet intervention and successfully contained a popular insurrection, Gero, in panic, called upon the Soviet army garrisons stationed in Hungary to rescue him from an outraged people. This decision, in turn, gave the revolt the character of a Hungarian-Soviet war under the impact of which the Hungarian Communist Party, unlike the Polish one, virtually disintegrated.

In a belated effort to salvage a desperate situation, Nagy was again made Premier during the night of October 23-24. Yet in marked contrast to Gomulka's tough insistence on accepting leadership only on his own clearly defined terms, the unfortunate Nagy allowed himself to be elevated to formal authority under obscure circumstances which failed to crystallize into anything suggesting a sense of national victory or vindication. The initial intervention of the Soviet garrisons which went on for four days proved both politically and militarily disastrous. It infuriated the Hungarian nation and undermined Nagy's fragile attempt to work out a viable "national Communist" solution for Hungary. Worse still, it led to the revolt of the Hungarian army and the formation of anti-Soviet and anti-Communist Workers Councils by workers throughout Hungary. Last but not least, it failed to crush the revolt. In desperation, the Soviet leaders again sent Mikoyan to Budapest on October 27 to strike the same kind of bargain which had been agreed to with Gomulka in Warsaw a week earlier. The Soviet army was to be withdrawn and Nagy given a chance to rally support on the basis of a "national Communist" solution. This move, however, came too late. The Hungarian freedom fighters' appetite was only whetted by this seeming Soviet retreat. The Hungarian Roman Catholic Primate, Jozsef Cardinal Mindszenty, released from confinement on October 30, declined to emulate his Polish counterpart and withheld support from Nagy. The latter, driven by the pressure of events and the logic of his own thinking during his years of forced retirement and disgrace, abandoned his attempt to balance on the thin edge of "national Communism." First he decided to restore the multi-party system of the years 1945-1947 (October 30), then to withdraw Hungary from the Soviet bloc (October 31), and finally to proclaim her neutrality under United Nations protection (November 1).

These moves the Soviet Union simply could not tolerate lest they trigger the dissolution of its entire power position in East Central Europe. Partly screened by the simultaneous Anglo-French and Israeli assault on the Suez Canal, which deflected world attention from events in Hungary, they launched a second and more massive military offensive against the Hungarian revolt which they inevitably crushed despite international protest and fierce Hungarian resistance. They also installed a new Communist regime under Janos Kadar, who had himself suffered imprisonment under Rakosi and who had therefore neither identified with the hated former

Party chief nor was inclined to emulate the independent course of Imre Nagy. The latter took refuge in the Yugoslav embassy in Budapest on November 4, but was abducted by Soviet military personnel when he emerged on November 22 despite a safe-conduct given by the Kadar regime. After long imprisonment and a secret trial he was executed a year and a half later during the night of June 15-16, 1958. Though perhaps an ineffectual Communist politician, Nagy's integrity, humanity, honesty, and martyrdom have made him a national hero.

The overriding significance of the Hungarian revolt lies in the fact that every presumed pillar of Communist power—the Party, the workers, youth, the intelligentsia, and the armed forces—proved wholly unreliable at the moment of showdown. Loyalty to the leadership, respect for the ideals of Communism, solidarity with the Soviet Union, proved nonexistent. The government was shown to have ruled only through coercion and fear. The revolt also punctured the myth of totalitarian invulnerability to erosion and rebellion. Smashed by superior force, it has still left behind a residue of national pride and laid bare the coercive and alien character of Communist rule. Incidentally, it occasioned disillusionment with the United States which, having initially encouraged the peoples of East Central Europe to work for and eventually to expect "liberation," did not, as widely expected, aid the revolt in any tangible way.

In Hungary itself, the Kadar regime over several years slowly restored order, rebuilt the Communist Party, granted amnesties to most of the revolutionaries, and finally resumed its economic development with yet another five-year plan for 1961-1965 after having been a massive economic liability to the USSR and the recipient of much economic and financial aid over several years. It cannot, however, live down the stigma of its origin and is thus a standing affront to national memory and pride. The general public is politically apathetic; the bureaucracy has lost its militancy and maintains a neutral stance between Party and people; the intellectuals live in a state of spiritual emigration. In an attempt to ease the bitterness which still lingers, Kadar moved to expel both Rakosi and Gero from the Hungarian Party after the Twenty-second Soviet Party Congress, even though both men have lived in exile in the USSR since 1956. He also granted a final amnesty for those revolutionaries still held in jail in 1963. Nevertheless it is symbolic of the national mood and ominous for the future that since 1959 abortions have exceeded live births.

In recent years much of the apparent quiet has been purchased by the regime through virtual economic bribery. Real income was said to have risen 34 per cent between 1956 and 1962, and the Eighth Congress of the Communist Party, in November 1962, reaffirmed the official intention of supplying every third household with a TV set and two out of every five with an electric washing machine by 1965. Ironically, this "frigidaire socialism" and "technical fetishism" has been vainly deplored both by the remaining Hungarian Stalinists and the humanistic idealists who for different reasons regret the apparent indifference and even cynicism toward political issues and social problems which characterizes both the governmental and the public mood. It remains to be seen whether further economic growth will lead to a wider distribution of material prosperity among the masses or simply reinforce existing class privileges.

Agriculture remains in difficulty due in part to poor weather and shortages of machinery, and also to the flight of young farmers to the cities. The depletion of labor power in the countryside has, in fact, been such that collective farms are offering generous share-cropping arrangements to the aging peasantry. Like her neighbor Rumania, Hungary has lately shown an awakening interest in trade with the Western world, especially those countries outside the European Common Market, such as Great Britain, Austria, Greece, Cyprus, and Japan as well as the developing nations. The European Common Market itself is watched apprehensively not only because its members take 10 per cent of Hungary's exports and account for 13.5 per cent of her imports but also for the potential threat they pose to Hungary's developing interests in Africa and elsewhere.

Albania and the Sino-Soviet Rift

CHAPTER NINE

Small and poor but strategically located, Albania was occupied by Italy in April 1939, and enlarged under Italian patronage by the assignment to her of Albanian-populated districts of Yugoslavia when the latter was dismembered by the Axis Powers in April 1941. During the war, nationalist and Communist resistance movements were organized, the latter sponsored by the Yugoslav Partisans sent into Albania by Tito in late 1941. Attempts in the summer of 1943 to achieve unity between the two movements proved abortive. Though desired by Albanian public opinion and urged by a British military mission, such unity was desired by neither the Yugoslav nor the Albanian Communist leaders. When, after Mussolini's fall, the German army replaced the Italian occupation force in September 1943, some nationalist resistance leaders began to cooperate with the Germans whose concessions to Albanian nationalism were quite generous. This collaboration provided the Communist resistance movement with grounds for launching a civil war against its nationalist rivals, a war from which the former emerged victorious in November 1944, soon after the Germans had withdrawn.

The Albanian Communist leaders, operating within a broader pattern familiar to the rest of East Central Europe, began their work within a seemingly innocuous Albanian Democratic Front, which held elections to a constituent assembly on December 2, 1945. Official statistics would have it that 92 per cent of the electorate had voted and that 93 per cent of the ballots had been cast for the Democratic Front. On January 11, 1946, a People's Democratic Republic was proclaimed and during February the Democratic Front was effectively purged of its non-Communist elements.

At this point friction between some Albanian Communist leaders and their Yugoslav mentors emerged as the former began to resent Yugoslav tutelage and to suspect Marshal Tito of wishing to transform Albania into a Yugoslav sub-satellite. Belgrade, for example, did not wish Albania to enter into diplomatic relations with the United States and also wanted to control Albania's relations with the Soviet Union. There was economic friction which the Albanians ascribed to Yugoslav exploitation while the Yugoslavs indignantly professed to major sacrifices on behalf of the ingrate Albanians. There was also the matter of Albanian resentment at having to return to Tito Albanian-populated territory which the Axis had assigned to Albania in 1941.

It is therefore not surprising that the Albanian

Communists, led by Enver Hoxha, should have used the occasion of the Tito-Stalin split in June 1948 as an opportunity to emancipate themselves from Yugoslav domination and to assert their own parity with the other People's Democracies. In the process, Hoxha executed the chief Titoist protégé and his own personal rival, Interior Minister Koci Xoxe. Ever since, the bulk of the Albanian Communist leadership has, for defensive reasons, not only remained rigidly Stalinist but has also been largely recruited from the Tosk people of Southern Albania. The north Albanian Gheg clans, which had traditionally dominated the southern Tosks, have been relegated to the political background, especially as the Albanians in Yugoslavia are also Ghegs and because Tito has sought to conciliate them with extensive political, economic, and cultural privileges in the Kosmet Autonomous Region of Yugoslavia, including a university at Pristina and higher living standards than their kinsmen in Albania enjoy.

In view of this background of national and personal enmity, which has had long-standing political, ethnic, ideological, and strategic implications, it was inescapable that Hoxha and the Albanian regime should have become alarmed when Nikita Khrushchev undertook his visit of reconciliation to Yugoslavia in May-June 1955 and launched his attack on Stalin in February 1956. In Hoxha's eyes, Stalin remained a hero who had enabled Albania to gain her independence from Tito. Would Tito's price for renewed amity with Khrushchev now be Hoxha's political head? Would Khrushchev pay that price as he had already done in Hungary with Rakosi's removal from power? How ominous was the fact that Soviet ideological specialists M. A. Suslov and P. Pospelov, attending the Third Congress of the Albanian Communist Party in April and May 1956, had urged Hoxha to rehabilitate posthumously his executed Titoist rival?

Then, to Hoxha's great relief, came the Hungarian revolt of October-November 1956, which led to a quick deterioration in Soviet-Yugoslav relations as Khrushchev held Tito's influence partly responsible for the debacle and clearly resented the Yugoslav refusal to accept the official version of events. Hoxha was apparently saved for a second time. Moscow's *Pravda*, the newspaper of the Soviet Communist Party, on November 8, 1956, published an article by him denouncing Tito. On November 13, 1956, he announced the execution of three "Titoist spies." He defended Stalin in a speech on February 13, 1957, to the Central Committee of the Albanian Communist Party and a few weeks later visited Moscow where, in April 1957, the Soviet government transformed its earlier economic credits to Albania into an outright gift of 422 million rubles.

During 1959 and 1960, however, when Khrushchev resumed his overtures to Tito once more and, after subduing an "anti-Party" group in his own Politburo, returned to his de-Stalinization policies, Soviet-Albanian relations cooled once again. This time, however, a new patron was available to Hoxha as the Chinese Communist leadership, for reasons of its own, also disapproved of Khrushchev's "revisionist" heresies. Thus Hoxha, who in 1948 had eluded Tito's grasp to enter Stalin's embrace, now jettisoned Khrushchev for Mao Tse-tung for whom, in turn, it was important to acquire a European ally, however small, to demonstrate that the Chinese were not alone or isolated within the Communist world.

The first public revelation of ideological dissension and political tension within the bloc was the failure of Hoxha to attend the Third Congress of the Rumanian Communist Party in June 1960, which developed into a general conference of leaders of the various Communist governments. Khruschev chose this occasion to proclaim as obsolete the venerable Communist doctrine of the inevitability of war between the Communist and "bourgeois" worlds. The Chinese demurred and the Albanian Communist Party newspaper *Zeri i Populit* had the temerity to edit Khruschev's speech in such a way as to omit a crucial passage.

Three months later, Hoxha was again absent when the other Communist bloc leaders accompanied Khruschev to New York in September 1960 to attend the fifteenth session of the UN General Assembly. The Albanians were snubbed by other Communist delegations while Khrushchev was almost ostentatiously cordial to Tito. Back in Albania, Hoxha ignored a Soviet embassy reception on September 12, 1960, honoring Albanian-Soviet Friendship Month. Then came the general meeting of eighty-one Communist parties in Moscow in November 1960, at which Hoxha referred to Khrushchev as a traitor, weakling, and revisionist. The enraged Khrushchev in turn vowed that Hoxha would be forced someday to wipe off "the bucket of filth" which he had hurled at the Soviet ruler.

It now appears that Khrushchev had during 1960 attempted to engineer one or more abortive *coups* to unseat Hoxha. This is suggested by the arrest, in July of that year, of Albanian Rear Admiral Temo Sejko who appeared to have had particularly close connections with the Soviet authorities. The execution of Sejko and three accomplices in May 1961 significantly coincided with the Soviet navy's evacuation of its Albanian submarine base at Sazan on the Adriatic Sea; and there was something less than convincing in the official charge that Sejko had plotted against Hoxha on behalf of the United States, Yugoslavia, and Greece.

Meanwhile, on September 8, 1960, Hoxha had also dismissed and arrested the two Albanian political leaders most closely identified with the Soviet Union: the wartime heroine and veteran Albanian Politburo member Liri Belishova and the former ambassador to Moscow and later president of the Central Audit Commission, Koco Tashko. In November 1960, Hoxha removed Belishova's second husband, Maqo Como, from the Agriculture Ministry. Thus, it is not surprising that when a new Soviet ambassador arrived in Albania in January 1961, he was icily received, especially since Khrushchev had accompanied his efforts at the internal subversion of Hoxha's authority with barely veiled external threats such as, for instance, his promise to a Greek neutralist politician to "look into" the question of autonomy for the Greek minority of southern Albania, which was not only an affront to Hoxha but also to Albania's national integrity.

The Fourth Congress of the Albanian Communist Party, meeting from February 13 to 20, 1961, was remarkable both for its adulation of Hoxha and for the sharp clash between P. Pospelov of the USSR and Li Hsien-nien of Communist China on the issue of peaceful coexistence with the capitalist world. Following this Congress, the Soviet Union, Czechoslovakia, and East Germany launched an economic blockade of Albania while China, despite her own economic troubles, jumped into the breach by shipping 91,000 tons of wheat and extending a loan of 500 million old (112.5 million new) rubles to Albania under the terms of a trade agreement signed in April 1961.

At the Twenty-second Congress of the Communist Party of the Soviet Union, Khrushchev openly attacked and Chou En-lai defended Hoxha and the Albanian Communist leadership in regard to their policies and ideological standpoints. Like Stalin in his campaign against Tito in 1948, so now Khrushchev, in turn, appealed for a popular and Party revolt against Hoxha who, like Tito, was in turn given the opportunity to pose as a national hero defending his brave little country against Great Power coercion and a plot to dismember her. Hoxha was also able to invert Khrushchev's attacks on "the cult of personality" when the USSR broke off diplomatic relations with Albania in December 1961. In consequence of all this Hoxha's prestige among Albanians is now such that Tito himself has been placed on the defensive at least insofar as he has found it prudent to grant even more autonomy to the Yugoslav Albanians of the Kosmet region lest they become actively irredentist.

It is, of course, the Sino-Soviet dispute and Mao's patronage that have made possible Hoxha's defiance of Khrushchev which, in turn, has exacerbated the rift and now makes Albania something of an independent variable in the present period of internal discord within the Communist world. The Chinese are certainly unlikely to abandon their Albanian protégé lest other Communist parties lose confidence in Peking's power and integrity. Yet Hoxha, hardly wishing to put all his eggs in one basket, has already sought to fortify his independence by extending feelers to the West. This development has gained added interest with the recent French recognition of Peking and perhaps, as much as any other, confronts the West with the need to clarify its interests and objectives with respect to the entire East European orbit during the present phase of internal tension within the world Communist movement.

Prospects and Problems

CHAPTER TEN

The Communist world in general, and the states of East Central Europe in particular, have undergone and continue to experience profound change since the nadir of Stalinist totalitarianism. Though the ruling Communist parties continue to monopolize state-political power, and though certain "classic" Communist economic policies and institutions remain obligatory, the earlier rigidity resulting from slavish imitation of the Soviet model in virtually all political, economic, cultural, and administrative matters has been significantly moderated and frequently abandoned. Terror has abated; the Stalinist isolation of the states of East Central Europe from the West and from each other has been relaxed; spoliation by the USSR, irrational economic behavior, and bureaucratic tyranny have all been reduced. Finally, the shock of the Polish and Hungarian crises of 1956 together with the subsequent Sino-Soviet rift have cracked the earlier monolithic solidity of the Communist bloc and given the East European states an opportunity to experiment with local divergences from the Soviet pattern.

The 1956 crisis, on the one hand, defined the limits of permissible political deviation for the People's Democracies. The Poles and Hungarians, and, by example, the other peoples of East Central Europe, learned the triple lesson that they are too weak to break out of the Communist camp by their own efforts; that the United States is not inclined to risk a major conflagration to help them do so; and finally that the Soviet Union is, in a showdown, prepared to use force to maintain the Communist regimes of the area in power. Hence, future revolutionary crises are less likely to originate in East Central Europe, where these lessons of 1956 have been absorbed, than they are in the Soviet Union itself, where possibly certain structural and ideological contradictions, sharpened by the political embarrassments following from the Sino-Soviet rift, will be brought into focus during an eventual succession crisis following the departure from the political scene of N. S. Khrushchev. The discrepancies between Marxist utopian promises and Soviet practice, between the messianic futurism of Soviet rhetoric and the conservatism of her bureaucratic apparatus, between the promises of affluence and the shabbiness of daily economic existence, are among these potentially revolutionary "inherent contradictions" of the Soviet system.

While such speculation must for the time being remain purely hypothetical, there is no denying the hard reality that the Sino-Soviet rift has given the People's Democracies of East Central Europe considerable leverage to achieve a maximum of local autonomy, short of outright defection. Today, within an increasingly polycentristic Communist camp, the East European regimes can maneuver between the two giants of the Communist world or (what appears to be more typical) they can (and have) extracted concessions from Moscow in return for supporting the Soviet protagonist. The Chinese, for their part, will not again help the Soviet Union to restore its own control over East Central Europe as they once did after the crisis year of 1956 which, in turn, tends to reinforce the need for more concessions by Moscow, both political and economic. Indeed there is a reciprocal relationship between these two categories as the Soviet Union seeks to compensate for greater political looseness within the bloc by working to retain control through greater economic integration. The latter, however, is proving to be both expensive and, perhaps, somewhat futile in policy terms. Stalinist exploitation of East Central Europe has had to be replaced by Soviet economic aid. What the more fragile or truculent "satellites" get as a prop and a bribe must also be given to the more docile ones by way of reward. Yet the Soviet Union is unlikely to have an inexhaustible stream of surplus capital and raw materials available to give the East European countries in the near future. Furthermore, the increasing national-political autonomy of the recipients results in a tendency among them to resist one of the corollaries of such Soviet aid as is granted, which is the pressure to synchronize and integrate their economies with each other and with the Soviet

Union. Instead, they look with covetous eyes on Western European trade outlets and view with anxiety a European Common Market which may close these outlets.

As its instrument of economic integration, the Soviet Union has revived and sought to strengthen the bloc's Council for Economic Mutual Assistance (CEMA). Founded in 1949 but largely moribund under Stalin who used it only as a tool of Soviet exploitation and to carry on his feud with Tito's Yugoslavia, CEMA has, since the mid-1950's, strained mightily to further economic integration of the People's Democracies along the lines of a genuine division of labor, economic rationality, and independence of non-Communist sources of supply. Whether, however, the member countries can be persuaded to cooperate to this extent without excessive Soviet coercion is becoming increasingly dubious. Furthermore, whether the essentially inward orientation being fostered by CEMA really supplies the answer to East Central Europe's long-run economic needs also remains an open question. Though helping to boost trade between the USSR and the People's Democracies from $1.9 million in 1950 to $6.7 billion in 1961, CEMA has failed to achieve area-wide economic integration. There is little mobility of capital and less of labor among the member nations. While Czechoslovakia, East Germany, and Poland have indeed launched some joint development projects, no member state has actually abandoned any significant sector of its own national economy. Each fears to be caught short as the result of a neighbor's production bottleneck. Thus, for example, a few years ago CEMA suggested that Poland limit her production of generators to those of 25-megawatt capacity and that the production of larger ones become the monopoly of the Soviet Union and Czechoslovakia. The Polish authorities have, however, disregarded this recommendation—which they apparently suspect as discriminatory—and have affirmed their intention to produce units of up to 120 megawatts and larger in the belief that any industrial nation of 30 million people must control and therefore produce its own power installations. This may be taken as typical of the manner in which national prestige and technological ambition limit and frustrate CEMA's and Soviet desire to achieve a division of labor and of production functions among member countries.

Lest, however, the erroneous conclusion be drawn that no economic cooperation at all takes place in East Central Europe, mention should be made of the current construction of an oil pipeline from the Soviet Union to Czechoslovakia, East Germany, Hungary, and Poland which is scheduled to have an initial capacity of eight million tons annually and an eventual one of twenty. An area-wide electric and telephone grid is also in an advanced stage of construction.

Quite apart, however, from the issue of multilateral integration, each of the Communist states suffers from local economic malfunctions and shortcomings. For one thing, population increases make imperative a speedy and sharp increase in agricultural output to avert a politically intolerable decline in living standards. This requirement, however, is one which the collective-farm system has chronically shown itself to be incapable of achieving. Yet, all of the Communist regimes, with the notable exception of Gomulka's Poland, are ideologically and administratively too committed to the alien and usually unworkable institution of the collective farm to be able to scuttle it without a disastrous loss of prestige.

The agricultural dilemma is paralleled by that of "economic crime" in industry. Thanks to persistent commodity shortages, unrealistic price systems, abuse of power by the elites, and resulting social demoralization, the Communist economies are wracked by pilfering, embezzlement, bribery, black-marketeering, and slovenly workmanship on a fantastic scale as massive quantities of materials are illegally diverted into clandestine production and marketing channels. This is perhaps the ironic nemesis of bombastic Communist propaganda concerning "socialist property" and "socialist morality."

Since 1956 the seeming primacy of economic issues in East Central Europe has resulted in a general public "withdrawal" from political concerns into something close to crass materialism as the masses direct their personal aspirations exclusively toward those goals which can be immediately and palpably gratified. It is problematical whether and for how long the Communist cadres themselves can avoid being drawn into this whirlpool of apoliticism.

Just as the new notion of "polycentrism" within the Communist camp rejects the earlier dogma of total Soviet control over other Communist parties and governments, so does the ideology of "revision-ism" deny the binding nature of the Soviet political, economic, and administrative structures as models for the states of East Central Europe. Revisionism and polycentrism thus become ideological tools with which the People's Democracies can seek to carve out for themselves freedom to experiment with original or indigenous styles of politico-economic organiza-tion and method. The Soviet form of society, argue the revisionists, was built in a backward agrarian environment, traditionally ruled by an absolute au-tocracy inexperienced in Western political traditions. Hence its institutions cannot be regarded as impera-tive prototypes for countries, such as those of East Central Europe, whose historical conditioning has been quite different. In the hands of the revisionists, the de-Stalinization campaign launched in 1956 was thus used to erode the moral authority of the Soviet Union within the bloc. Started as a repudiation of Stalin's terror system, revisionism has developed an intellectual momentum of its own in consequence of which a number of its spokesmen have gone beyond the original attack on Stalinist practice to a rejection of Lenin's theory of the monolithic Party and a few have even passed on to a denial of Marx's historical materialism. All the revisionists demand greater in-ternal democracy within the Communist parties and a return to the moral content of socialist theory. Most of them appeal for more intellectual freedom and scrupulous adherence to standards of objective truth in place of party-line rhetoric. Some of them also insist that a multi-party system is not incompatible with socialism which might, they hope, indeed benefit from a revitalization of free parliamentary discussion. The irony of the revisionist position is that its spokesmen, precisely because of their continuing concern with political, and particularly with socialist, ideas and ideals, are hardly representative of the materialistic-minded masses who seem generally to share the bureaucratic *apparat*'s contempt for the "abstract" values of intellectual freedom.

It may be asked if it is in the interest of the United States, the West, and world peace that these various trends toward domestic relaxation and loosened ties between members of the Communist bloc be encouraged to deepen and widen. If so, then it would appear to follow that those East European Communist leaders who have asserted their independence of Moscow, including, in their different ways Tito, Gomulka, and Hoxha, ought to receive Western support, either overtly or covertly, though their domestic policies may be unattractive or even highly distasteful. Such support might range from economic aid to diplomatic backing and recognition or acceptance of controversial political realities such as the Oder-Neisse line. Since the states of East Central Europe are increasingly anxious to expand their trade with the West, the latter may find it wise and useful to establish a unified agency to carry on such trade and to conduct it with the avowed political purpose of "rewarding" those countries and leaders who are prepared to assert and maximize their autonomy and independence from Moscow while also providing them with the economic leverage to do so.

In time, such Western support may well help to moderate some of the less attractive institutional features of these East Central European regimes, as eventually proved to be the case in Tito's Yugoslavia. It would, however, be illusory to expect these states to cease to be Communist. In any event, to withhold Western aid simply by way of "punishment" for being Communist will merely force the would-be "deviationists" back into the Soviet vise and discourage others from attempting to assert even a limited measure of independence. Western support, whether economic, diplomatic, or political, must not, of course, take the form of a blank check but always be conditional on the recipient's determination and actual capacity to achieve, defend, and widen this independence.

The political power of the East European Communist states relative to the Soviet Union may well expand thanks to a factor not yet critical but impossible to rule out in the future. In the event of a domestic Soviet succession struggle after the death or withdrawal of N. S. Khrushchev, the various contenders for power may find it necessary or expedient to bid for ex-"satellite" support, particularly if such competition should go on for a long time. The eventual victor in such a struggle may have to make important concessions to a Gomulka, for example, so as to obtain Polish Communist recognition of his personal primacy as well as backing in any major doctrinal conflict, whether or not that might involve an extension of the present Sino-Soviet dispute. Thus, whereas in the Stalin era Soviet power was omnipotent and Russian decisions politically beyond challenge in a group of satellite states whose aspirations and leading personalities played a negligible role, the next decade may well witness a situation in which East Central Europe will not only be more autonomous and display greater diversity, but may also have a significant impact on Soviet domestic politics.

Reference section designed by Witt-Francis Associates and produced by Maryart Stu

Part II

Reference

prepared by Rudolf L. Tokes

contents

POLAND

CZECHOSLOVAKIA

HUNGARY

RUMANIA

YUGOSLAVIA

BULGARIA

0   150   300

SCALE IN MILES

ALBANIA

Eastern Europe in Facts and Figures

Table 1 Eastern Europe in Facts and Figures (1962)

Country	Area Sq. Miles	Population	% Urban	% Rural	Illiteracy
Albania	11,100	1,625,378	15*	85*	20-25%*
Bulgaria	42,729	7,905,000	33.5	66.5	10-15%*
Czechoslovakia	49,366	13,745,300	57.5	42.5	1.7
Hungary	35,919	10,050,000	40.3	59.7	3.0
Poland	120,359	30,133,000	48.5	51.5	3.0
Rumania	91,699	18,566,932	31.3	68.7	10-15%*

*Approx.

Table 2 Religious Composition after World War II

ALBANIA (estimated)

Moslems	65.0%
Greek Orthodox	23.0
Roman Catholic	11.0
Other	1.0

BULGARIA

Eastern Orthodox	84.4%
Moslems	13.5
Roman Catholics	.8
Jewish	.06
Other	1.6

CZECHOSLOVAKIA

Roman Catholic	69.0%
Protestant	8.0
Czech Church	7.0
Greek Orthodox	.4
Jewish	.4
Uniate	1.0
Without confession	14.2

HUNGARY

Roman Catholic	67.0%
Calvinist	22.8
Lutheran	3.3
Greek Orthodox	2.5
Jewish	1.5
Other	2.9

POLAND

Roman Catholic	95.02%
Eastern Orthodox and Protestant	4.0
Jewish	.08

RUMANIA

Orthodox	79.1%
Uniate	8.0
Roman Catholic	6.0
Protestant	5.0
Jewish	1.0
Other	0.9

Map of Territorial changes following World War II

Pomerania
E. Prussia
White Russia
POLAND
Silesia
Bessarabia

Before

After

ROMAINIA

Dobruja

Table 3   National Minorities of Eastern Europe

ALBANIA		BULGARIA		CZECHOSLOVAKIA	
Albanians	95.00%	Bulgarians	87.00%	Czechs	66.50%
Greeks	2.00	Turks	6.00	Slovaks	28.00
Vlachs	2.00	Macedonians	4.00	Magyars	3.10
Serbs (approx 1000)		Gypsies	2.00	Germans	1.20
		Other	1.00	Poles	.60
				Ukrainian/Russians	.60

HUNGARY		RUMANIA		POLAND	
Magyars	94.0%	Rumanians	86.6%	Poles	96.9%
Germans	2.25	Magyars	9.0	Ukrainians	.7
Gypsies	1.75	Transylvanian Germans	2.0	Byelorussians	.7
Yugoslavs	1.0	Gypsies	1.5	Russians	.8
Slovaks	0.85	Ukrainian/Russian	.5	Gypsies	.5
Rumanians	0.15	Tatar, Turks, Bulgars	.2	Germans	.5
		Serbs, Croats, Slovenes	.2	Lithuanians	.08
				Slovaks	.06
				Czechs, Greeks	.03

POLAND

CZECHOSLOVAKIA

German

Czech

Slavakia

HUNGARY

RUMANIA

YUGOSLAVIA

BULGARIA

0   150   300
SCALE IN MILES

ALBANIA

	Poles		Bulgarians
	Magyars		Rumanians
	Czechs		Turks
	Slovaks		Greeks
	Albanians		Germans

99

Table 4 — Principal Press Organs of Communist Eastern Europe

Name	Description	Circulation
ALBANIA		
Drita	Newspaper of Albanian Writers and Artists Union	N.A.
Rruga e Partise	Theoretical monthly of CC	N.A.
Zeri i Popullit	Party daily	N.A.
BULGARIA		
Septemvri	Organ of Writers' Union	31,200
Novo Vreme	Monthly theoretical organ of Party CC	33,500
Rabotnichesko Delo	Daily central Party organ	500,000
Trud	Trade Union daily	110,000
Narodna Mladezh	Daily Komsomol organ	223,000
Otechestven Front	Fatherland Front daily organ	200,000
CZECHOSLOVAKIA		
Rude Pravo	Czech Party daily	1,048,621
Pravda	Slovak Party daily	278,021
Nova Mysl	Czech Party theoretical monthly	85,998
Mlada Fronta	Czech Youth Federation organ	130,000
Plamen	Literary monthly of Writers' Union	
Praca	Czech Trade Union daily	220,000
Prace	Slovakia Trade Union daily	250,000
HUNGARY		
Nepszabadsag	Hungarian Party daily	730,000
Tarsadalmi Szemle	Hungarian Party theoretical monthly	35,800
Nepszava	Trade Union daily	35,800
Magyar Nemzet	Daily of the Patriotic People's Front	35,800
Magyar Ifjuság	Weekly of the Communist Youth League	35,800
POLAND		
Nowe Drogi	Theoretical monthly of Party CC	100,000
Glos Pracy	Trade Union daily	35,000
Polityka	Warsaw weekly	N.A.
Trybuna Ludu	PUWP daily — official party organ	300,000
Prasa Polska	Monthly of Association of Polish Journalists	N.A.
Kultura	Organ of Polish Writers' Union	N.A.
Sztandar Mlodych	Polish youth organ	97,000
Slowo Powszechne	Daily of "PAX" group	100,000
Dziennik Ludowy	UPP daily	N.A.
Wies Wspolczesna	UPP theoretical monthly	N.A.

Name	Description	Circulation
	RUMANIA	
Scinteia	Party daily	920,000
Lupta de Clasa	CC theoretical monthly	N.A.
Viata Romineasca	Writers' Union literary monthly	N.A.
Munca	Trade Union daily	N.A.
Scinteia Tineretului	UTM daily	305,000
Romina Libera	Organ of the People's Councils	232,000
Gazeta Literara	Writers' Union weekly	232,000

Table 5 Books and Daily Newspapers of Communist Eastern Europe (1961)

	Number	Circulation	#/1000 Population	Book Titles Published
Albania	2	74,000	5	388
Bulgaria	12	1,585,000	200	3,181
Czechoslovakia	24	3,710,000	269	9,728
Hungary	23	1,522,000	152	5,672
Poland	46	4,492,000	150	7,224
Rumania	33	2,986,000	161	6,456

Table 6 East European Radio and Television

Country	No. of Radio Receivers	No. of Television Receivers	No. of TV Stations	Hours of TV Broadcasting per week
Albania	60,000	300	—	—
Bulgaria	1,601,000	31,000	1	approx 20-25
Czechoslovakia	3,621,000	1,300,000	11	51
Hungary	2,430,000	404,000	8	39
Poland	5,487,000	1,000,000	16	46½
Rumania	2,165,000	88,000	5	27½

Table 7 East European Monetary System and Exchange Rates

Country	Currency	(DOLLAR VALUE — AUGUST 1960) Rate of Exchange Official	Tourist	Free Market Western Europe
Albania	Lek	50.00	—	—
Bulgaria	Lewa	6.80	9.52	23.79
Czechoslovakia	Crown	7.20	14.35	28.12
Hungary	Forint	11.74	23.30	47.84-50.76
Poland	Zloty	4.00	23.94	88.56
Rumania	Lei	6.00	12.00	25.38

 The Communist Parties

1. Introductory remarks on party membership statistics
2. Table 1. Number and social origin of party members [1947/48-1962]
3. Table 2. Size of the Communist parties of Eastern Europe in percent of total population
4. Table 3. Overlapping Party-Government membership [June 1963]
5. Table 4. The Communist Party of Czechoslovakia — membership
6. Table 5. The Communist Party of Czechoslovakia — leadership
7. Table 6. The Hungarian Socialist Workers Party — an organizational chart [December 1962]
8. Brief histories of:

   a. The Communist Party of Albania [1940-61]
   b. The Communist Party of Bulgaria [1903-44]
   c. The Communist Party of Czechoslovakia [1921-44]
   d. The Communist Party of Hungary [1918-44]
   e. The Communist Party of Poland [1918-44]
   f. The Communist Party of Rumania [1921-44]

Communist Party Membership: A Short Note.

Stalin once classified the Communist Party members into "generals, officers, and noncommissioned officers." This characterization not only points up the genuine military character of the party as opposed to Communist pretensions concerning "intra-party democracy," but also corresponds to the numerical distribution of the cadres at the upper, middle, and lower echelons. The respective figures for the East European parties are approximately 0.02 — 3.98 — 96 percent for any given party's total membership.

The first two categories indicate the numerical strength of full-time paid party officials (members and staffs of central, regional, district, and local party committees) and the third is the rank and file, duty-bound to engage in part-time unpaid party work as assigned by the "generals" and the "lieutenants."

The changing social composition of the Communist parties is shown below. Due to differing methods of computing the class background of party members (some parties classify their membership according to class status as acquired by birth, others according to current profession) it is impossible to obtain a precise picture, although a few trends are clearly discernible.

The most conspicuous fact is the decline in the number of workers in the parties of the more industrialized states of Poland, Czechoslovakia and Hungary and an increase in the less industrialized countries including Albania, Bulgaria and Rumania. The corresponding increase in white collar membership is often disguised as party functionaries are often listed as workers by birth. Similarly, the Party's well known cadre shortages in the countryside are not truly reflected in official figures, since there are fewer party members among the peasantry in fully collectivized Czechoslovakia than in Poland which has virtually no collectivized farms.

The growth in the number of white collar workers, party bureaucrats, professionals and members of the armed services is a clear indication of rising educational standards, industrialization and modernization in the hitherto agrarian societies of Eastern Europe. This process of "de-proletarianization" is likely to result in a series of parties officially still labeled "proletarian" but essentially composed of the "new middle class" of an embourgeoised Eastern Europe.

Polish Party and government leaders Cyrankiewicz, Gomulka and Zawadski addressing mass rally after the "October Days" of 1956.

Table 1 — Communist Parties

Country	Membership 1962	Peasants 1947-48	Peasants 1962	Workers 1947-48	Workers 1962	White Collar Workers* 1947-48	White Collar Workers* 1962
Albania	53,659	66.9	70.00	19.7	30.0**	13.4	
Bulgaria	615,000	43.8	34.16	25.9	37.16	30.3	30.71
Czechoslovakia	1,680,819	31.0	48.1	57.0	49.1	12.0	42.8
Hungary	511,965	37.3	19.0	56.0	40.5	6.7	40.5
Poland	1,310,525	22.1	11.8	57.3	40.3	20.6	47.9
Rumania	1,100,000	39.0	29.0	44.0	47.0	17.0	26.18

*May include two or more of the following categories: Party officials, members of government bureaucracy, members of military and police forces, professionals, scientists, artists, housewives and pensioners

**Includes party and government officials and members of the armed services

Table 2 — Size of Communist Parties of Eastern Europe as Percent of Total Population*

Country	1938	1948	1962
Albania	0.0	3.8	4.25
Bulgaria	0.4	6.3	6.68
Czechoslovakia	0.5	21.0	12.22
Hungary	0.3	10.9	5.08
Poland	0.06	6.0	4.34
Rumania	0.006	6.3	5.92

*Figures for 1938 and 1948 taken from R. V. Burks, The Dynamics of Communism in Eastern Europe, Princeton University Press, 1961, p. 51.

Table 3 — Overlapping Party-Government Membership (June 1963)

Country	Number of Politburo Members and Candidates	Number Holding Government Post Also
Albania	15	7
Bulgaria	12	7
Czechoslovakia		
Czech Party	11	7
Slovak Party	11	6
Hungary	19	9
Poland	11	4
Rumania	14	11

Imre Nagy, first appointed Hungarian Premier in April 1953 to implement the "New Course" following Stalin's death, is shown here addressing the parliament.

Table 4

Membership in the Communist Party of Czechoslovakia —

December, 1962

Number of members 1,535,978
Number of candidates............. 121,043

          Total.................1,657,021
= 12.1% of the total population
  17.5% of those over 18 years of age
Number of Primary
  Organizations........................ 45,907

Party membership as % of those over 18 years of age comprises:
      20.2% in the Czech regions
      11.0% in Slovak regions

Party membership according to sex:
      72.8% male
      27.2% female

Length of Party membership:
    Joined before 1945 .... 1.0%
      between 1945-47 ....37.2%
      between 1948-52 ....28.7%
      between 1953-57 ....11.0%
      between 1958-61 ....22.1%

Number of individuals expelled from the Party since 1946:
  June 1946 - January 1947........177,000
  Fall 1948 - January 1949 107,133
  May 1949 - June 1954.............401,520
  1954 - 1957 151,590
  1958 - June 1962 63,172

        Total.........900,415

Source: **Zivot Strany,** February 1963

Table 5

The Leadership of the Communist Party of Czechoslovakia —

December, 1962

Central Committee
Number of Full Members.... 97
Number of Candidate Members....... 50
         Average age: 55 years

Length of Party Membership of CC Members and Candidates:

Joined the Party before 1945............ 47
          since 1945............ 73
          since 1946............ 13
          since 1947............ 3
          since 1948............ 6
          since 1950............ 5

Social Composition of CC Members and Candidates:

  Workers 85
  Peasants 2
  White collar workers................... 24
  Professionals [intelligentsia] 22
  Others 14

Present Occupation of CC Members and Candidates:

  Party organs 41
  State administration 39
  Industry 23
  Agriculture 7
  Mass organizations 11
  Science 16
  Army and police........................... 7
  Health 3

National Origin of CC Members and Candidates:

  Czech 115
  Slovak 29
  Hungarian 1
  Ukrainian 1
  Polish 1

Table 6

Hungarian Socialis

(after the 8th C

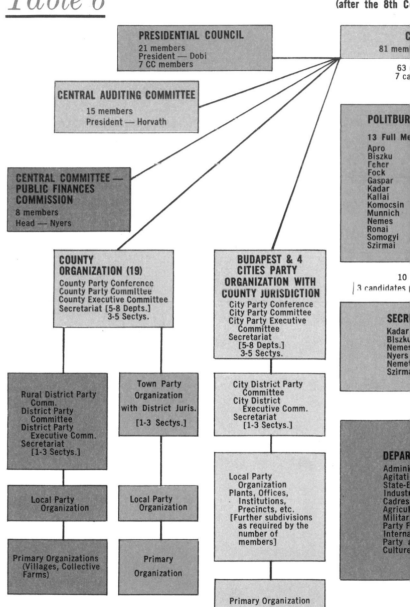

PRESIDENTIAL COUNCIL
21 members
President — Dobi
7 CC members

C
81 mem

63
7 ca

CENTRAL AUDITING COMMITTEE
15 members
President — Horvath

POLITBUR

13 Full Me

Apro
Biszku
Feher
Fock
Gaspar
Kadar
Kallai
Komocsin
Munnich
Nemes
Ronai
Somogyi
Szirmai

CENTRAL COMMITTEE — PUBLIC FINANCES COMMISSION
8 members
Head — Nyers

10
3 candidates

COUNTY ORGANIZATION (19)
County Party Conference
County Party Committee
County Executive Committee
Secretariat [5-8 Depts.]
3-5 Sectys.

BUDAPEST & 4 CITIES PARTY ORGANIZATION WITH COUNTY JURISDICTION
City Party Conference
City Party Committee
City Party Executive Committee
Secretariat
[5-8 Depts.]
3-5 Sectys.

SECR
Kadar
Biszku
Nemes
Nyers
Neme
Szirma

Rural District Party Comm.
District Party Committee
District Party Executive Comm.
Secretariat
[1-3 Sectys.]

Town Party Organization
with District Juris.
[1-3 Sectys.]

City District Party Committee
City District Executive Comm.
Secretariat
[1-3 Sectys.]

DEPAR
Admini
Agitati
State-E
Industr
Cadres
Agricul
Militar
Party F
Interna
Party a
Culture

Local Party Organization

Local Party Organization

Local Party Organization
Plants, Offices,
Institutions,
Precincts, etc.
[Further subdivisions as required by the number of members]

Primary Organizations
(Villages, Collective Farms)

Primary Organization

Primary Organization

Party (M.S.Z.M.P.)
er 1962)

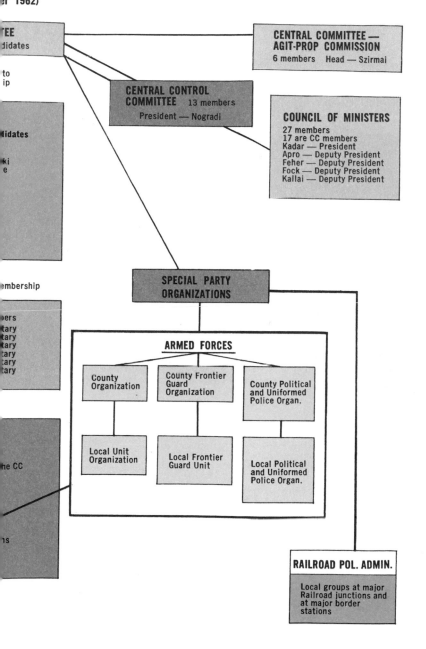

TEE
didates

to
ip

**CENTRAL COMMITTEE —
AGIT-PROP COMMISSION**
6 members   Head — Szirmai

**CENTRAL CONTROL
COMMITTEE** 13 members
President — Nogradi

Midates

ki
e

COUNCIL OF MINISTERS
27 members
17 are CC members
Kadar — President
Apro — Deputy President
Feher — Deputy President
Fock — Deputy President
Kallai — Deputy President

embership

pers
tary
tary
tary
tary
tary
tary

he CC

**SPECIAL PARTY
ORGANIZATIONS**

ARMED FORCES

County
Organization

County Frontier
Guard
Organization

County Political
and Uniformed
Police Organ.

Local Unit
Organization

Local Frontier
Guard Unit

Local Political
and Uniformed
Police Organ.

RAILROAD POL. ADMIN.
Local groups at major
Railroad junctions and
at major border
stations

ns

The Communist Party of Albania

In 1924, after a Yugoslav imposed government assumed power in Albania, a few leftist students went to Moscow and joined a committee affiliated with the Balkan Confederation of Communist Parties which functioned under Comintern control. Of the original "hard core" of three Albanian Communists in Moscow composed of Maleshova, Fundo and Kelmendi, the last returned to Albania in 1930 to organize Communist cells. Later some members of the group took part in the Spanish Civil War and, when World War II broke out, emissaries of the CP of Yugoslavia set out to organize a Communist Party in Albania. They found four small warring groups sharply divided by tribal, social, and ideological differences. Nevertheless the Albanian CP was founded on November 8, 1941 as a result of a merger of three of these groups. After three years of successful partisan activities, and generous aid from British and Yugoslav sources, the Party found itself alone in the political arena at war's end.

After four years of semi-independent existence as a Soviet-sub-satellite under Yugoslav control, party chief Enver Hoxha regained his autonomy following the Soviet-Yugoslav split and launched a full-scale anti-Titoist campaign in the course of which he liquidated his internal enemies headed by Koci Xoxe. By 1949 Albania had become a full-fledged Soviet satellite deriving about 38 per cent of its state revenues from loans and grants from Soviet bloc countries.

After Stalin's death in 1953 and especially as a result of moves toward Soviet-Yugoslav reconciliation after 1955, the danger of renewed Yugoslav interference and the possibility of a withdrawal of Soviet support loomed ominously over the super-Stalinist Albanian leadership. As in 1948 however, when Albania was perhaps saved from possible Yugoslav annexation by the latter's expulsion from the Cominform, the Hungarian revolution of 1956 again seemed to prove the correctness of the Albanian Party's "hard line" and thus permitted continuation of its Stalinist policies. As a result of subsequent Soviet preoccupation with the political stabilization of the bloc and Khrushchev's struggle with an "anti-party" group, the Albanian party managed to remain a relatively free agent to pursue its own policies with less than usual regard for Soviet wishes.

In the course of ensuing intrabloc ideological debates the Albanian leadership found itself increasingly in agreement with the views of the Communist Party of China concerning questions of peace, coexistence and war.

Between the spring of 1958 and the end of 1959 the Albanian Party associated itself with the Chinese on no less than 20 selected issues then being discussed within the world Communist movement. The Albanian views were made even clearer when they were seen to coincide with those of China on the occasion of the Moscow Declaration of 81 Communist Parties in December 1960. Since then Albania has made a more or less complete break with the USSR and maintains only scant relations with the rest of Eastern Europe. A beneficiary of Chinese ideological, political, and economic help it is today "Chairman Mao's Adriatic outpost."

The Communist Party of Bulgaria

Among the Communist Parties of Eastern Europe the Bulgarian is the oldest. It was founded by Dimitri Blagoev who, like Lenin, insisted on the elite character of the party which remained "narrow" in terms of membership and popular support until the Russian Revolution of 1917.

A charter member of the Comintern, Blagoev's group formed itself into the Communist Party of Bulgaria in 1919. It took part in the parliamentary elections in the same year, and became the second largest party next only to the Agrarians. The party's dogmatic leadership, guided by appropriate Comintern instructions, refused to support the genuinely popular Stambulisky government and stood aloof when the Agrarians were overthrown in 1923. In an attempt to rectify this tactical mistake, the party joined the radical Agrarians and participated in an abortive revolt in September 1923. Following the "September Events" the party leaders, Georgi Dimitrov, Vasil Kolarov and Valko Chervenkov fled to the Soviet Union, formed a "Politburo Abroad" to guide the party's home activities and took leading positions in the Comintern. Despite an ill-advised and unsuccessful terrorist bomb plot against the King organized by the party in 1925 which claimed the lives of 150, the outlawed Bulgarian Communists were allowed to reorganize in 1927 as the Independent Workers Party, ran in the elections of 1931 and obtained 31 of 274 parliamentary seats. Although the party's membership never exceeded 30,000 it consisted of a determined group of intellectuals, civil servants, students, and militant trade unionists, thus constituting the strongest Communist Party in the Balkans.

In 1934 when all political parties were banned, the Communists went underground and, in 1936, formed a "popular front" with an agrarian radical group. In the summer of 1942 the party started organizing the Fatherland Front, which engaged in resistance and traditional terrorist activities against politicians of pro-Nazi sympathies. On September 9, 1944 with the help of the Soviet Army the Communists organized a coup d'etat and took over the government.

The Communist Party of Czechoslovakia

The Communist Party of Czechoslovakia was founded by left-wing dissident members of the Czech Socialist party in 1921. Unlike other Bolshevik-inspired parties of the area, the Czech party was a legal contender for political power in Eastern Europe's "only functioning democracy" during the inter-war years and enjoyed appreciable mass support. The party polled nearly a million votes in 1923 and consistently maintained its electoral strength (41 deputies in 1925, 30 in 1929 and 30 again in 1935) which always exceeded its actual membership.

A late joiner of the Comintern, it took considerable prodding by the Soviet representative to have a leftist majority elected at the Second Party Congress in 1924. During the next five years a new type of leadership — thoroughly Bolshevik and blindly loyal to Moscow — grew up comprising such figures as Gottwald, Slansky, Kopecky and Zapotocky. This well organized team of Muscovites achieved its objective in 1929 when it succeeded in purging the "rightist opposition" at the Fifth Party Congress. Although the fully Stalinized party did lose a sizeable portion of its membership, fear of the Nazi danger returned many defectors to the Communist fold during the 1930s.

Although plagued by the mushrooming of "leftist" and "rightist" deviationist groups, Gottwald and his colleagues firmly held the reins making the Czech party one of the more reliable members of the Comintern. During the Soviet purges the Czech leadership watched the gruesome Moscow proceedings from their safe haven in Prague and lost few if any of their key members.

Communism in inter-war Slovakia was less important but more complex than in the Czech lands The Slovak leadership included the native "DAV" group led by Clementis and others, the "1919'ers," veterans of the short-lived Slovakian Soviet Republic of that year, including the ethnic Hungarian, pro-Czech Siroky, the Magyarized ethnic-German Jewish Ferenc Munnich (now member of Kadar's Politburo in Hungary) and a number of then little known faithful Slovak *apparatchiki*.

The Munich crisis of 1938 found both Communist parties well organized and determined to oppose the Nazi intruders. This forthright attitude, in strong contrast to President Benes' wavering in the face of imminent invasion, gained the party additional supporters and was remembered by the electorate during the balloting at the first postwar elections in 1946.

During the German occupation the Communists played a leading part in resistance activities, carried on successful partisan raids from the mountains and generally constituted the only organized group willing and capable of fighting the Germans in a resolute manner. The anti-German Slovak uprising of 1944, led by nationalists and Communists, represented another major gain on the political balance sheet.

The Communist Party of Hungary

The party was founded in November 1918 by former Hungarian prisoners-of-war returning from Russia with Bolshevik instructions, by members of a Socialist anti-military youth group, and by several left-wing members of the Hungarian Social Democratic Party. After a few months of skillful organizational and propaganda activities led by Bela Kun under Lenin's personal guidance, the party, joined by the Social Democrats, formed the Hungarian Soviet Republic on March 21, 1919. Due to lack of popular support, however, and military defeats suffered at the hands of numerically superior armies of the neighboring Successor States, the Kun regime fell after 133 days of existence.

Admiral Horthy's regime which followed systematically repressed the few remaining Communist underground cells and, in fact, rendered all Communist activity futile during the next twenty years. The exiled Hungarian Communist leaders found employment as officials of the Communist International, editors of left-wing publications in Western Europe and in the United States, and as activists in the Communist parties of Austria, Germany and France.

The Nazi takeover of Germany drove most of these exiles to Moscow after 1933 where, during the great purges, many veteran Hungarian Communists, including Kun himself were liquidated or sent to forced labor camps. In 1936 the Comintern also dissolved the party's Central Committee both in Hungary and in the Soviet Union.

By 1941, the party began to recuperate from its losses and attempted to resume its clandestine activities in Hungary. This, however, proved to be extremely difficult, since, as the story goes, the chief of Horthy's political police knew every one of Hungary's three hundred leading Communists by name and invariably arrested them after their first careless move. As a result, Communists did not and could not distinguish themselves in any organized wartime resistance movement and emerged — aside from the obvious advantages derived from the presence of the Red Army — as weak junior partners in the first postwar coalition government. Shortages of trained personnel, the stigma of being associated with the ill-remembered "bloody Commune of 1919" and with the brutality of the "liberating" Soviet troops were the Party's most characteristic problems when it began its uphill struggle for political hegemony in 1945.

The Communist Party of Poland

The Communist Party of Poland was founded by the pro-Russian Social Democrats of the Kingdom of Poland and Lithuania (SDKPiL) and by dissident members of the Polish Socialist Party on December 16, 1918. A charter member of the Communist International, the Polish Party became the most closely controlled foreign ally of the Soviet party. Its subsequent activities included the organization of some strikes, the illegal publication of newspapers and brochures, and isolated acts of terrorism.

After boycotting the elections of 1919 the Party succeeded in electing two deputies in 1921, and again in 1922. By 1925, with the help of assorted cover parties, the Communists had 18 deputies in the Polish legislature. Plagued by incessant intra-party struggles, leaders of various factions very often asked Moscow to arbitrate disputes among them. This invariably invited purges, and in the thirties the liquidation of those found to have deviated from the current Soviet party line.

After the Pilsudsky coup d'etat of 1926 — which the Party ironically supported — and especially following 1928, the government's repressive measures greatly reduced Communist influence and party membership as well. This was followed by probably the most traumatic experience in the party's history; its entire leadership whether residing in Moscow or enticed by Stalin to go to the Soviet Union "for consultations" was murdered to the last man during the great purges of 1936-38.

In 1938 the Comintern dissolved the Communist Party of Poland "for being contaminated by hostile elements ... where agents of Polish fascism managed to gain positions of leadership." Although these charges were patently untrue, and were officially admitted to have been such in February 1956, the result was that by 1940 only those Polish Communist leaders were alive whom the Polish government had obliged by keeping imprisoned during the Soviet purges.

With the help of instructors sent from Moscow, the Party was slowly reorganized during the first years of the war. After the Soviet break with the Polish government-in-exile, Stalin officially threw support to an adequately "purified" Polish Communist leadership, which subsequently evolved into the Lublin Committee, the first post-war government of Poland.

The Communist Party of Rumania

The Rumanian Party was established in 1921 by a group of Social Democrats after their own party refused to join the Communist International. During the years of its legal existence, the Party engaged in extensive agitation among industrial workers and frustrated religious and disenfranchised national minorities which Rumania acquired after the Paris Peace Settlements of 1919-20. Faced with the threat of a Communist dominated Trade Union Council, the Liberal government outlawed the Party in December 1927.

Official suppression, however, did not end, but only curtailed Communist activities in Rumania. The Party carried on uninterrupted propaganda among the minorities, participated in two of the country's traditionally manipulated elections in 1927 and 1932 under the name of the Workers' and Peasants' Bloc and thus generally managed to hold its own until the early 1930's when the repercussions of the worldwide economic crisis gave new impetus to Communist activities, especially among organized industrial workers.

In 1933 the party led a particularly effective political strike at the Grivita railroad workshop, whereupon King Carol's secret police opened a frontal attack, determined to uproot the last vestiges of Communism in Rumania. After thorough police work the party, with its entire leadership imprisoned, local cells destroyed, and funds exhausted virtually disintegrated by the end of 1936. The Iron Guard Fascist dictatorship which followed King Carol's monarchical dictatorship no less than General Antonescu's wartime government both pursued anti-Communist activities with equal zeal, thus reducing the party, very much as in the case of Hungary, to a few hundred desperate activists at the time of the arrival of Soviet occupation forces in August 1944.

A Communist Party congress in session.

③ Communist Personalities

Brief Biographies of:

Enver Hoxha

Born into a middle class Moslem family in 1908. As a recipient of a state scholarship, he spent the years 1930-1936 in France. Abandoned his studies, went to Paris, joined various Communist discussion groups and worked for an editor of the Communist newspaper *L'Humanité*. After his recall to Albania he spent four years as French teacher in high schools. Became prominent among local Communists, and one of the Albania Party's founders, a member of the first Central Committee, and was elected as temporary Secretary General. Hoxha was a leader of the KORCE group and was instrumental in the liquidation of two other groups contending for Party leadership. By 1943 Hoxha had consolidated his position as leader of the Army and the Communist-run National Liberation Movement and emerged as Albania's first postwar Prime Minister in 1944.

An enthusiastic supporter of Stalin's anti-Yugoslav policies, Hoxha purged one of his former supporters Sejfulla Maleshova in 1946 and his potential rival Koci Xoxe, Minister of Interior and head of Secret Police, in 1948. During the next ten years Hoxha held as many as six positions simultaneously in Party and state. As a staunch opponent of de-Stalinization, continued a one-man campaign of attrition against his colleagues in the Party. In 1961, Hoxha was the only surviving member of the original group of 14 wartime Albanian leaders, while the Party's 43 member Central Committee was packed with Hoxha's various relatives, numbering some 25 people. Because of personal and ideological differences stemming from his unwillingness to de-Stalinize and follow Khrushchev's policy of reconciliation toward Yugoslavia, Hoxha has, in recent years, allied his Party with the Chinese Communists.

Mehmet Shehu

Son of a village mullah, was born in 1913. After completing five years of elementary school, attended the American Vocational School in Tirana and graduated in 1932. After his expulsion from an Italian military college for Communist activities, Shehu returned to Albania and attended an officer's school in Tirana. During the Spanish Civil War he joined the Garibaldi International Brigade and became an acting Battalion Commander. By then a member of the Spanish Communist Party, spent three years in a French internment camp. In 1942 joined the Italian Communist Party, returned to occupied Albania and organized one of several resistance groups. As a Hoxha protégé, he soon rose to the rank of Major General in the partisan army. In 1945-46 attended the Voroshilov Military Academy in Moscow and upon his return was named Chief of Staff of the Albanian Army. Because of his bitter anti-Yugoslav feelings Shehu experienced a series of rapid demotions in 1948 and was only saved by Tito's excommunication from the Soviet bloc in June 1948.

Shehu's career took a sharp upward turn after 1948. He was appointed Minister of Interior, Vice Premier, Member of the Politburo and Secretary of the Party Secretariat and thus became second only to Hoxha. Gave up his post of Secretary in 1953 and was appointed Premier in 1954, a position he continues to hold.

Todor Zhivkov

Son of poor peasants, was born in 1911. After some years in elementary school went to an art school, then worked for the State Printing Office in Sofia. In 1930 joined the underground Communist Youth Organization and two years later became a member of the Communist Party. Slowly worked his way up in the Party hierarchy and became the leader and organizer of regional resistance activities in 1943.

In 1945 was elected candidate member, then in 1948 full member of the Party's Central Committee. After 1948 Zhivkov gained control over the capital's Party and government organizations. From this power base he rose to the Politburo-candidature and Secretaryship of the Central Committee in 1950. In 1951 was elected a full member of the Politburo and in 1954, at the Sixth Bulgarian Communist Party Congress Zhivkov was elected First Secretary of the Central Committee, replacing Vulko Chervenkov under the new post-Stalin policy of collective leadership.

With a remarkable display of political durability Zhivkov has managed to remain on the top since 1954. In November 1962 the former Stalinist Zhivkov engineered the expulsion from the Party or the demotion of most of his potential rivals and solidified his position as the undisputed leader of the Bulgarian Communist Party.

Anton Yugov

Was born in 1904 to poor Bulgarian peasants. After a few years of elementary school began to work in a factory. Formed the Communist Youth Organization in 1920. Took part in the September uprising of 1923 as an active member of the Macedonian Revolutionary Organization. Subsequently engaged in underground activities and joined the Party in 1928. In the following years served in various Party posts, interrupted only by a 15 month stay during 1934 at the Lenin School of the Communist International in Moscow. Elected to the Politburo, Bulgarian Communist Party in 1937, held several responsible positions in the Party apparatus. In 1941 Yugov escaped from internment and was appointed one of the Central Committee Secretaries in charge of armed resistance activities. From 1944-48 served as Minister of Interior and ruthless prosecutor of the democratic opposition. Yugov's influence declined somewhat in the years of 1949-54 but Chervenkov's attempt in 1950 to implicate him in the "Titoist" Traichko Kostov affair did not materially influence his position.

In 1954 was appointed First Deputy Premier and in April 1956 succeeded Chervenkov as Prime Minister. In November 1962 was expelled from the Central Committee and lost his government position "for crude violations of Socialist legality" presumably committed during his tenure as Minister of Interior.

Valko Chervenkov

Born in 1900 in a small village, son of a noncommissioned officer in the army. During his high school years Chervenkov actively participated in student strikes. Joined the Party in 1919. His organizing and journalistic talents earned him increasingly important assignments; Secretary of Sofia district and city Communist Youth Organization (1923) in charge of supplies and weapons, editor of underground Party paper (1923-25), member Central Committee, Bulgarian Communist Party (1925). After 1925 attended a Soviet military academy then the Marx-Lenin Institute in Moscow. Attained prominence in the Communist International and in 1937 became the Head of the Comintern's Lenin School. Supported by Georgi Dimitrov then Secretary-General of the Comintern, Chervenkov rose high in the Party hierarchy by the end of 1944. After the war he was appointed to the Politburo and the Central Committee, edited the Party's theoretical monthly and in 1948 was elevated to the Central Committee Secretariat. Became Deputy Prime Minister in July 1949 and Premier a half year later. In November 1950 was appointed

Secretary-General of the Central Committee, thus concurrently holding the highest Party and state positions of the country.

After Stalin's death Chervenkov was forced to give up his exalted Party post in 1954 and was replaced as Premier by Zhivkov in April 1956. Less than a year later Chervenkov lost the Deputy Premiership and in June 1958 was divested of his post as Minister of Education. In late 1961 he was dismissed from the Politburo and a year later at the 8th Congress of the BCP was expelled from the Party for "crude violations of Socialist legality" and for creating "an atmosphere in the Party alien to Marxism-Leninism."

Klement Gottwald

Son of Moravian Catholic parents. At the age of twelve was sent to Vienna to learn the carpenter's trade. In Vienna he came under the influence of Socialism and acquired a fair knowledge of literature and Marxism. After World War I he took part in Socialist activities and in 1921 joined the newly founded Communist Party. As a successful editor of a provincial Communist newspaper he was elected to the Party's Central Committee in 1925 and also became the head of its Agitation and Propaganda department. The next stage in Gottwald's career was his election to the Comintern's Central Executive Committee at its Sixth Congress in 1928. Then with appropriate support from Moscow he set out to wrest control from the "Right" wing of his own Party. After considerable intrigue and the use of ruthless methods he succeeded in "Stalinizing" the Party by 1929. Prominent in the Comintern, he took part in preparing its Popular Front strategy in 1935. In that year he was also elected deputy to the Czechoslovak National Assembly in Prague.

Having spent the war years in the Soviet Union, Gottwald returned to his homeland as the leader of a powerful Communist Party. He served as Deputy Prime Minister from April 1945 to July 1946; Prime Minister from July 1946 to June 1948; and President of the Republic from June 1948 to March 1953.

Owing to his governmental duties, Gottwald retained only the Party Chairmanship and relinquished the General Secretaryship to Rudolf Slansky at the Eighth Party Congress in March 1946. This move proved to be unwise. By the late forties Slansky had grown to be a powerful opponent with a rudimentary organization of his own, threatening Gottwald and his followers with isolation. Gottwald engineered Slansky's downfall methodically. First he forced the purge of some of Slansky's followers in lesser Party positions. Then he maneuvered his opponent into a position where he was obliged to defend his discredited friends. On the very day of Slansky's downfall Gottwald absorbed the Secretary Generalship into his own Party Chairmanship. Gottwald died ten days after Stalin's death on March 14, 1953 presumably due to pneumonia acquired while serving as Stalin's pallbearer.

Antonin Novotny

Born a bricklayer's son in 1904. Joined the Social Democratic Party while an apprentice locksmith and the Communist Party in 1921. During the next ten years Novotny worked in various Communist-led youth organizations and was sent to Moscow as a delegate to the VIth Congress of the Comintern in 1928. In the thirties he gradually rose in the Party hierarchy: first as the Chairman of the Party organization of a Prague suburb, then as an instructor for the Prague regional Party organization and later as Secretary of the Prague district. Following underground Party work conducted during the first years of Nazi occupation Novotny was arrested and sent to the Mauthausen concentration camp in 1941.

After the end of hostilities, Novotny was named First Secretary of the Prague district, a position which he held until 1951, and was also elected to the Central Committee in 1946. Novotny, thought to be the leader of young Party bureaucrats who helped to depose Slansky, obtained Slansky's seat in the Secretariat and Politburo at the end of 1951 and was Deputy Prime Minister in January 1953. The timely death of President Gottwald in March 1953 helped Novotny to become the Party's First Secretary in September 1953. He became President of the Republic himself when he succeeded Antonin Zapotocky. Following the 22nd Soviet Congress and especially after the Czech Party Congress of December 1962 the inveterate Stalinist Novotny reluctantly embarked upon a belated de-Stalinization program which was only just gaining momentum during 1963.

Viliam Siroky

The son of a worker, he began as a railroad laborer at the age of thirteen. Became involved in Socialist activities and joined the Communist Party in 1921. During the twenties, distinguished himself as an able organizer in Slovakia and was rewarded by being named a delegate to the Comintern Congress of 1928. Siroky was elected to the Central Committee and became an ally of Gottwald at the decisive Party Congress in 1929. Imprisoned several times between the two wars, he was elected as a Communist Deputy to the National Assembly in 1935 and in the same year attended the Seventh Comintern Congress in Moscow. Before Munich, Siroky served as Bratislava District Communist Secretary and was in charge of the Slovak Party organization before being forced to leave for the Soviet Union in 1938. After three years of clandestine Party work, he was arrested in 1941 in Slovakia and spent the rest of the war in prison.

Siroky became Deputy Prime Minister in the first postwar government and Chairman of the Slovak Communist Party. In 1949 he was elected to the Politburo of the Czechoslovak Party in recognition of his efforts to bring about the integration of the Slovak and Czech lands. He became Prime Minister in 1953, a position he held until September 1963 when he was dismissed from this post for "certain mistakes in his past political activity," i.e., prosecuting Slovak Communists in the early fifties and complicity in Vlado Clementis' execution, and was replaced by Jozef Lenart, a young Slovakian Party bureaucrat.

Matyas Rakosi

Born in 1892, son of a small town shopkeeper. One of the most promising students at the Budapest Commercial Academy, Rakosi joined a Socialist youth group in 1911. Before the war, spent two years in Hamburg and studied in London. Captured by the Russians in 1916, organized leftist Social Democratic circles in Siberian prisoner-of-war camps. In 1918 joined Bela Kun's group in Moscow, became a member of the Russian Communist Party's Hungarian section as well as a Soviet citizen. Returned to Hungary in November 1918, was a founding member of the Communist Party of Hungary. During the Hungarian Soviet Republic of 1919, the 27-year-old Rakosi was appointed Deputy People's Commissar for Commerce and Transportation, and later Commissar for Production and, as such, was the youngest member of the Kun government. After the fall of the Commune he fled to Austria, then went to Moscow and joined the Comintern as an "international instructor." In the latter capacity Rakosi supervised the activities of the Italian and French Communist Parties between 1920-24. In 1925, while on an underground mission, was captured in Budapest, tried and sentenced to an eight and one-half year jail term. In 1935 was retried and received a life term. Shortly after the Stalin-Hitler Pact, Rakosi was freed and sent to Moscow in exchange for certain military memorabilia captured by Tsarist troops in 1849. As one of the senior leaders of the Party (who had lived through the Moscow purges in a Hungarian jail) Rakosi rose to the top in the Party. He returned to Hungary with the advancing Soviet troops and was elected Secretary General of the Party in December 1944. As the leader of one of the four coalition parties he held the position of Deputy Prime Minister between 1945 and 1952. An accomplished theoretician, brilliant and ruthless strategist, and inventor of the Party's famous "salami tactics," he had just claim to call himself "Stalin's most eminent Hungarian disciple." Drawing upon the Soviet Party's experiences, Rakosi wellnigh completely eliminated his entire actual or potential opposition within the Party between 1948 and 1952. With Imre Nagy's rise to power Rakosi was forced to give up his government post of Prime Minister, but retained his Party position as First Secretary. After the 20th Soviet Party Čongress, Rakosi steadily lost ground and, at Moscow's insistence, was forced to resign on grounds of ill health in favor of Erno Gero in July 1956.

Living in exile in the Soviet Union since October 1956, Rakosi was expelled from the Party in August 1962 for his responsibility for the execution of "innocent Party members" and voicing "groundless suspicions against...leaders of other fraternal parties" and thus causing "immeasurable damage on the international scale." From the latter charge, it could be surmised that Rakosi, besides being an old anti-Titoist, might have been involved in the activities of the Soviet "anti-Party" group in 1957. Rakosi was reported dead in August 1963.

Imre Nagy

Born of a peasant family in 1896. Joined the metal workers' union at the age of eighteen. Drafted into the army and captured by the Russians in 1916. Once freed, he joined the Russian Red Army and the Russian Communist Party and served in one of the "internationalist" divisions until late 1920. Returned to Hungary in 1921, enrolled in the Social Democratic Party on instructions from the Communist Party. Was arrested and tried in 1927 as a leader of a shortlived crypto-Communist Party. In 1930 at the 2nd Congress of this illegal party, held in Vienna, Nagy gave the Central Committee's report on agriculture. Recognizing Nagy's expertise and talents on agrarian questions, the Comintern appointed him a research associate in Bukharin's International Agrarian Institute in 1930. Little is known about Nagy's activities during the following years in Moscow except for a few articles on agrarian economics and the fact that he survived the Soviet purges despite his association with the executed Bukharin.

During the war Nagy worked as an editor with Radio Kossuth, the Hungarian language Soviet propaganda station. Although at odds with Rakosi and Revai due to the "nationalist" overtones of his radio programs, Nagy returned to Hungary in 1944 as a reliable member of the Party's unified Muscovite group. Nagy as the Minister of Agriculture in the first postwar government gained great popularity as the man in charge of distributing the land among poor peasants. His physical appearance — mustached, speaking with the accent of his country and his down-to-earth personality — clearly set Nagy apart from his Muscovite colleagues.

After six months as Minister of Interior, Nagy was named Speaker of Parliament, elected to the Politburo in 1948 and appointed Minister of Crop Collections in 1951. In 1951 he became a member of the Party Secretariat and in November 1952 was appointed Deputy Prime Minister.

Nagy reached the summit of his political career in June 1953 when he took over the Premiership from Rakosi to become the main architect of the post-Stalin "New Course" in Hungary. After Malenkov's fall in February 1955, Rakosi made a quick comeback, had Nagy removed from the government and subsequently expelled from the Party. Nagy attempted to fight back with a series of memoranda addressed to members of the Central Committee. Through these writings (published in 1957 in English under the title "On Communism") Nagy gradually developed the ideology of "National Communism" — a set of views which later served as fighting slogans in the spring and summer of 1956. The restoration of Nagy's Party membership in October 1956 came too late to forestall the snowballing events which subsequently pushed the reluctant Nagy into the leadership of the Hungarian Revolution.

After a five month long secret trial, Imre Nagy was hanged on the morning of June 17, 1958.

Janos Kadar

Born in 1912, son of a laborer. Joined a Communist-oriented youth group at the age of seventeen. Elevated to the youth organization's Central Committee and joined the illegal Communist Party in 1931. In the Party Kadar worked under the direction of Laszlo Rajk, the man whom he later helped to send to the gallows by luring him into a confession of Titoism and nationalist deviation in 1949. In the 1930's Kadar was arrested and jailed twice for Communist activities. During the war he was co-opted to the illegal Party's Central Committee and in 1943 was named its Secretary in charge of organizing anti-Nazi movements. In the spring of 1945, Kadar was promoted to the Politburo as a compromise candidate between the Muscovite and "Hungarian" factions. From May 1945 until June 1948 Kadar served as Secretary of the Budapest Party organization, and was elected Deputy Secretary General in November 1946 and again in June 1948.

Following Rajk as Minister of Interior he proved to be a faithful Rakosi-man until his own arrest in 1951 as a "Rajkist and Titoist." After a three year prison term, during which he underwent torture similar to those he had applied when in charge of the police, he was released, readmitted to the Party and appointed District Secretary of one of the industrial suburbs of the capital.

In July 1956 Kadar was readmitted to the Central Committee and replaced Gero in the Party Secretariat in October 1956. During the Revolution Kadar joined and supported the Nagy government only to abandon it in the first days of November 1956. With Soviet help he established a Cabinet and assumed the leadership of the renamed Hungarian Socialist Workers' Party. He gave up his government post in January 1958 but resumed the Premiership in September 1961, a position which he again concurrently holds with his supreme Party post since October 1963. One of the most consistent de-Stalinizers in Eastern Europe, Kadar purged the remaining die-hards of his party in August 1962 and has become the undisputed leader of the Hungarian Party.

121

Wladyslaw Gomulka

Son of a skilled oil worker, Gomulka was born in 1905. At the age of 14 he became an apprentice locksmith. Active in Socialist Youth movements he joined the illegal Communist Party in 1926. Took part in strikes and suffered a bullet wound when arrested after the Lodz Strikes of 1931. Attended the Lenin Institute in Moscow between 1934-36. Was arrested upon his return to Poland. Was fortunate to be in jail when the rest of the Polish Communist leadership was liquidated in Moscow (1937-38).

Organized the Communist-led People's Guard resistance group in occupied Poland and led the fight against the Germans and some non-Communist resistance groups as well. In 1943 he became Secretary General of the Party and in 1945 First Deputy Premier in the government of the Soviet-sponsored Lublin Committee. Also was in charge of the recovered Western Territories, directed the expulsion of Germans and the Polonization of the area. Except for his unwillingness to imitate Soviet methods in economic policies blindly, Gomulka had a near-perfect Stalinist record.

Nevertheless, finding himself at odds with the Muscovite faction of the Party, his demotion was inevitable even before Tito's expulsion from the Cominform. In 1951 he was arrested and exiled to a country house. Released from jail in 1955 he returned to the political scene after the Poznan riots of June 1956. Gomulka had, by then, a well established image of a non-Muscovite moderate and emerged as the only Communist capable of rallying the masses behind the Party in a time of severe crisis. With the support of his predecessor, Edward Ochab, Gomulka was elected to the post of First Secretary of the Polish United Workers Party at the historic Eighth Plenum in October 1956. Enjoying the full support of the masses, he prevented a Russian armed intervention similar to the one in Hungary, instituted liberal measures, and reached a compromise with the Catholic Church. Since the Sejm (Parliamentary) elections of January 1957, in which the Polish United Workers Party won a near total majority with Cardinal Wyszynsky's support, Gomulka has become the undisputed political leader of Poland as well as the most influential East European spokesman in the councils of the Soviet bloc. Although in recent years many measures of political liberalization have been rescinded and intellectual non-conformity severely repressed, Gomulka has managed to maintain a middle course between the Party's liberals and extremists and to preserve many achievements of the Polish October.

Boleslaw Bierut

A son of a small farmer, born in 1892. At the age of 12 was expelled from school for taking part in an anti-Russian school strike. During the next several years he worked as a bricklayer, painter, and surveyor. From 1912 to 1919 was active in the cooperative movement and became a member of the Socialist Party. In 1919 Bierut joined the Communist Party and was later forced to flee the country to escape arrest for subversive activities. In the Soviet Union joined the Comintern and in 1926 returned to Poland as an organizer of this agency of international Communism. Arrested in 1927, he forfeited bail and went back to Moscow. As Comintern staff member he carried out assignments abroad between 1927 and 1931. After another two years of clandestine activities in Poland, he was arrested and sentenced to seven years in prison. During the German invasion in 1939 he escaped to the Soviet Union. At the end of 1943 Bierut was parachuted into Poland and became the Chairman of the Communist-sponsored underground parliament called the National Council of the Homeland. In September 1944 the Polish Committee of Liberation made Bierut Acting Head of State. Three years later the fraudulently elected Sejm (Parliament) named him President of the Republic. A member of the Party's Politburo, Bierut was chosen Secretary General after Gomulka's forced resignation in the Fall of 1948. Between 1948 and 1952, he concurrently held the highest State and Party offices. When the Constitution of 1952 abolished the former, Bierut replaced Cyrankiewicz as Prime Minister while retaining his Party post. Two years later Bierut prudently divested himself of the Premiership and kept his dominant Party position. As one of the practitioners of the Stalinist "cult of personality" his timely death in March 1956 prevented his probable disgrace and demotion following the 20th Soviet Party Congress.

Jozef Cyrankiewicz

Born in 1911 of middle class parents. Studied law at the University of Cracow, but did not graduate. In 1933 he became an active member of the Socialist Party. As a reserve artillery officer was taken prisoner by the Germans in 1939. Cyrankiewicz managed to escape and joined an underground Socialist organization. Arrested in 1941 by the Germans, he was sent to the Auschwitz death camp; while in the camp, joined a secret Communist cell. In 1945 he offered his services to a crypto-Communist wing of the Socialist Party and subsequently became the head of a Socialist group advocating close cooperation with the Communists.

In 1946 Cyrankiewicz signed an agreement establishing a united front between the Polish Socialist Party (PPS) and the Polish Workers' Party (PPR). Became Prime Minister after the elections of February 1947. During the next year he concentrated on bringing about the merger of the PPS and the PPR, which took place in December 1948. He was elected to the Politburo of the Polish United Workers Party. In 1952 he was forced to give up the Premiership but two years later reacquired the same position which he still holds.

During the decisive days of October 1956 Cyrankiewicz cast his lot with Gomulka and since then has remained the First Secretary's strong supporter.

Gheorghe Gheorghiu-Dej

Born in 1901 in Moldavia. First came to public attention in 1933 as a strike leader at a Bucharest railway workshop. Sentenced to twelve years in prison; the government refused to ex-change him for Rumanian politicians captured by Soviet troops during the occupation of Bessarabia in 1940. While in jail he improved his meager education and thus fortified was allowed by the Antonescu Government to escape from jail in 1944 as a gesture to the oncoming Red Army.

Gheorghiu-Dej was made Politburo member and elected Secretary General in 1945. In 1948 was named First Deputy Premier and was one of the signers of the Cominform resolution expelling Yugoslavia. Owing to his "neutral" background (worker, native born Rumanian, Gentile) and shrewd politics he avoided being purged together with Patrascanu, Luca, and Pauker and instead became Prime Minister in June 1952. A year later he also took over the post of First Party Secretary.

Sensing the change of Moscow's line from one-man to collective party leadership, Gheorghiu-Dej prudently relinquished his high Party post in 1954. A year later he gave up the Premiership and reacquired the Number One Party post. These steps, however, in no way diminished his power position in the Party and the government.

The events of October 1956 in Hungary were said to have strengthened his position in the Rumanian Party which was fearful of similar outbreaks among the country's sizeable national minorities. In the summer of 1957 the Rumanian First Secretary disposed of the last vestiges of his internal opposition, very much as Khrushchev was doing with respect to the Stalinist "anti-Party" group in the USSR.

Gheorghiu-Dej proved to be extremely successful in making

124

Rumania into a country with one of the fastest rates of industrial growth, not only in Eastern but Western Europe as well. Thus he enjoys a virtually unshakeable position in the Party, and occasionally can afford to oppose the Soviets on economic issues.

Ana Pauker

Born in 1893, the daughter of a Moldavian rabbi. Pauker played an important role in clandestine Communist activities during the 1920's. She was a Party leader in her own right when in 1932 her husband Marcel Pauker was Secretary General of the Party. Upon information received from her, Marcel Pauker was executed by the Soviet Secret Police for Trotskyite deviation during the purges. In 1936 she was sentenced to ten years in a Rumanian prison but was exchanged to the Soviets in 1940. Reputedly very close to Stalin, Pauker was a member of the Comintern's Executive Committee until it was disbanded in 1943.

After the war Pauker was a prominent figure in the Rumanian Communist hierarchy: member of the Politburo, Secretariat, and Central Committee, and after 1947 Minister of Foreign Affairs. By 1949 Mme. Pauker was also Vice Premier in the government. Sensing the growing strength of the anti-Semitic Gheorghiu-Dej group, she attempted to create a faction of her own. In 1952, however, she was dropped from both Party and government posts and is now reportedly working as a minor government official.

Vasile Luca

Born in 1898. One of the earliest members of the Party which he joined in 1922. Was imprisoned several times for Communist subversive activities between 1920 and 1940. During the war Luca lived in the Soviet Union and returned with the advancing Red Army in the summer of 1944.

After the war Luca rose to the very top of the Party and government: he became a member of the Central Committee, Politburo, Secretariat and of the powerful Organizational Bureau, in addition to holding responsible government positions as Vice Premier and Minister of Finance.

Although he remained unscathed in the anti-Titoist purges of 1948, in order to insure his political, if not indeed physical survival, Luca gradually allied himself with the Pauker-Georgescu faction in opposition to the increasingly powerful Gheorghiu-Dej. Handicapped by his Hungarian nationality background, Luca was no match for Gheorghiu-Dej's "all Rumanian" team. In 1952 he lost all his Party and government positions, and in 1954 was brought to trial and sentenced to life imprisonment as a "traitor to the working class."

1. A historical and functional note on East European purges under Stalin

2. A checklist of key purges in Eastern Europe

STALINIST PURGES

In 1934 Stalin declared that in the process of building socialism, neither class struggle nor hostile activities of classes disenfranchised by the victorious proletariat would cease. On the contrary, they would grow in intensity as the elements inimical to socialism became more desperate. This thesis heralded the coming of Stalin's Great Purges, which, except for a pause during World War II, lasted until his death in 1953.

According to Khruschev, this quasi-ideological reasoning was motivated by "Stalin's cult of personality." This euphemism, however, does not appear to be a full or satisfactory explanation for the imprisonment, deportation, and murder of millions of men and women in the Soviet Union and East Europe. Thus, the reasons for these ideologically sanctioned crimes must be sought elsewhere.

As a rule, a totalitarian one-party state cannot afford to tolerate the prolonged existence of opposition in any form, actual or potential, whether stemming from members of former hostile groups or parties or deviant Communist factions within the Party. Any such groups are seen as representing an extreme danger to the proletariat under conditions of alleged "imperialist encirclement." They are said to threaten its security, while it is engaged in the dual task of strengthening the Party's position in society and undertaking gigantic tasks of economic and social engineering. External insecurity coupled with the fear of internal opposition thus lead to a series of repressive measures within Communist states which periodically engulf not only those opposed to Communism but many of the ruling Party's hierarchy as well.

Between 1945 and 1951, 3000 publicly reported political trials took place in Eastern Europe. Since 90 per cent of the trials were conducted in secret, the toll in human lives is still uncounted. However, on the basis of available evidence it is fair to assume that during this period approximately 25,000 executions followed both the public and secret trials.

Discounting the prosecution of Nazis and Fascist sympathizers five types of trials were held in Communist Eastern Europe involving: (a) leaders of Socialist parties and Trade Unions; (b) leaders of agrarian and middle class parties; (c) religious leaders mostly of the Roman Catholic faith; and (d) various leading Communists in every Communist Party of Eastern Europe on charges of heresy, treason, etc.

This last group is the most significant, for an understanding of the predicament with which the East European Parties were faced after Stalin's death and more particularly after the 20th Soviet Party Congress of 1956 where Stalin's crimes were first denounced by Nikita Khrushchev.

There had been two more or less distinct purge periods in post-war Eastern Europe. The first (1944-47) eliminated many small "home-grown" Communist factions (Trotskyite, nationalist, etc.). After these accounts were settled, the Communist Parties displayed a facade of unity until early 1948, in an effort to overcome the resistance of other non-Communist Parties.

Tito's expulsion from the Cominform, however, opened the gates to the flood of intraparty purges that soon engulfed the Peoples Democracies. From this time on the systematic elimination of all non-Stalinist factions began and involved: (a) those who represented an actual or potential opposition group to the incumbent leadership who were now accused of sympathizing with Tito's heretical views on national independence; (b) those whose past record included cooperation (usually under Party orders) with socialist or bourgeois parties in the wartime resistance movements now charged with espionage and betrayal of the party; (c) veterans of the Spanish Civil War and of other Communist activities abroad now represented as espionage agents for Western imperialist powers; (d) leading Communists of national and religious minorities abruptly branded as "bourgeois-nationalist" deviationists; (e) miscellaneous artists, writers and professionals guilty of "opportunism."

Czechoslovak President Gottwald (center) with First Party Secretary Rudolf Slansky (left) and leader of the Trade Union movement (ROH) Zapotocky in 1950 before Slansky's dismissal, imprisonment and trial.

Almost none of these charges corresponded to the real facts and were later admitted to be lies and falsifications by the former Party prosecutors themselves. The political and psychological effects of the purges on the Parties' members and on the populations at large were, however, more significant at the time than were the accusations, and the individual victims.

Politically, the purge trials engendered an avalanche of denunciations which put the rank and file of the Party and the so-called "class aliens" at the mercy of the secret police. They also required humiliating and ostentatious displays of political reliability and ideological subservience. Psychologically, the purges destroyed the membership's faith in yesterday's heroes who suddenly became today's villains. Thus, they created a chaos of values by casting doubt on the credibility of charges leveled by the Party, injected a sense of personal insecurity and fatalism into the thinking of Party activists, and degraded the Communist political process to the level of intramural war of attrition in the eyes of the population.

The process of de-Stalinization and the rehabilitation of victims of the Stalinist purges began in 1954 and still has not been completed in East Europe. Poland and Hungary were the first to begin to restore the violated principles of "Socialist legality" by releasing Gomulka and his followers in Poland and Laszlo Rajk's surviving associates in Hungary.

Khrushchev's secret speech at the 20th Soviet Party Congress in 1956 denouncing Stalin's crimes gave a further impetus to the struggle against the remnants of the "cult of personality." The Polish and Hungarian events of that year, however, suggested the wisdom of caution and deliberate speed to the rather reluctant Czech, Rumanian and Bulgarian parties.

The Albanians have never initiated de-Stalinization and still hold Stalin's full record in high esteem. Although Khrushchev's struggle with the conservative anti-Party group and the Yugoslav-Soviet dispute of 1958-59 retarded de-Stalinization, the Rumanian and Bulgarian Parties had "cleansed" themselves by the end of 1961. This process, however, only began in Czechoslovakia at the end of 1962 and it may take some time before the Party's internal housecleaning is completed to Moscow's satisfaction.

Scene at the solemn re-burial of Hungarian Party leader and Foreign Minister Laszlo Rajk which marked his official rehabilitation on October 6, 1956.

A Checklist of Key Purges in Eastern Europe

Albania	1948 Koce Xoxe — former Minister of Interior, Member of Central Committee: tried and executed "for Trotskyite and Titoist activity." 1960 Liri Belishova — Secretary, Central Committee Albanian Workers Party· executed for "treasonable activities." None Rehabilitated
Bulgaria	1949 Traichko Kostov — former Secretary, member of Politburo, and Deputy Prime Minister: tried and executed for Titoism with several co-defendants. Rehabilitated in 1956
Czechoslovakia	1952 Rudolf Slansky — former Secretary General, CP of Czechoslovakia, and thirteen co-defendants tried and executed with ten others for "treason, bourgeois cosmopolitanism and Zionist activities." Partially rehabilitated in 1963 Vlado Clementis, former Minister of Foreign Affairs, and a group of Slovak intellectuals as co-defendants, tried and executed for "bourgeois nationalism." Fully rehabilitated in 1963
Hungary	1949 Laszlo Rajk, former Minister of Interior and Minister of Foreign Affairs, member of Central Committee, Hungarian Communist Party and 13 co-defendants: tried for "being agents of Western intelligence services and Titoist deviationists." Rajk and four others were executed. Rehabilitated in 1956
Poland	1951 Wladyslaw Gomulka and M. Spychalsky, Secretary Central Committee of Polish United Workers Party and Deputy Minister of Defense respectively, arrested for "nationalist deviation" and subsequently accused of "espionage and consorting with foreign imperialist agencies." Released in 1955 and rehabilitated in 1956
Rumania	1952 Vasile Luca and Ana Pauker, former Ministers of Finance and Foreign Affairs, ousted and demoted respectively for "left and right wing deviation, and counterrevolutionary bourgeois nationalism." Not rehabilitated

⑤ Mass Organizations

A Brief Functional Analysis of Mass Organizations

An Introduction to Mass Organizations

According to a recently published Soviet *"Handbook for Agitators"* the role of mass organizations in a state building socialism may be compared to the "transmission belts" of an intricate machine whose movements are defined by the motor serving as the power source.

In Communist states the task of these groups is to mobilize different strata of society for specific political, economic or social goals. This is accomplished through constant participation in and frequent exposure to political and economic campaigns initiated and controlled by the Party. They also serve as instruments of control which frustrate individual initiative and foster political and cultural conformity through systematic encroachment on the citizen's leisure-time activities. Finally, they provide the Party and the government with a vast reservoir of candidates to replenish the country's political and economic elites.

Of the four types of mass organizations listed below, National Fronts are the largest in size comprising between 60 and 99 per cent of a country's population over 18 years of age. National Fronts are wholly devoid of political significance. They are designed to mobilize the greatest number of electors to participate in all phases of a national election campaign including campaign meetings, discussion of candidates, and voting for the names selected by the leadership. Participation by other parties in elections whether national or local does not, however, imply that the Communist Party relinquishes any appreciable amount of its own political power. Rather, this subtle device is designed to provide the citizen with old party labels while *actually* voting for Communist policies.

Through compulsory trade union membership of all blue and white collar workers, the Party has effective control over wages, working conditions and the distribution of social and cultural fringe benefits. Although the days of frenzied "Stakhano vite" working competitions are past, the trade unions still have considerable leverage over the workers in matters of production speed-ups, adjustments of norms, wages, bonuses, no less than in the administration of vacation and health plans for entire industries, individual enterprises and institutions.

Although para-military organizations have lost much of their importance since the early fifties, they still represent a significant force as preparatory schools for the Soviet bloc's armies. Youngsters, desiring to fly an airplane, operate a short-wave radio or drive a car have no other choice but to join such groups. Here the emphasis is less on political indoctrination than on mastering some militarily useful skill.

Next to the Communist Parties, youth groups are the politically most significant mass organizations. It is not without significance that the supposedly Communist-controlled Hungarian Organization of Working Youth started the Revolution in October 1956, and that Polish student and youth groups threw their support behind Gomulka in the crucial days of 1956, subsequently becoming his most severe critics in trying to defend the freedoms won during the Polish October.

Not unlike the Soviet Komsomol, East European youth organizations are usually led by middle-aged Party members who are generally members of the Party's Central Committee. Rank-and-file members are subjected to intensive political and anti-religious indoctrination, and are required to relieve manpower shortages at collective farms and on highway construction and irrigation projects during weekends and summer vacations. Enthusiastic participation in this type of activity is usually a condition for admission to universities and institutions of higher learning. Like the Communist Parties, East European youth organizations suffer from chronic cadre shortages in the countryside. Lack of interest in organized political activities, great distances from urban centers, the relative absence of effective central control, often make these rural youth groups into song and dance clubs rather than bastions of Socialism.

Table 1 — Deputies Elected to the People's Councils in Poland

Party	No. of Councilors 1958	No. of Councilors 1961	% of Votes Received 1958	% of Votes Received 1961
PUWP*	83,070	83,360	40.5	45.3
UPP**	43,464	39,645	21.2	21.5
DP***	3,472	3,670	1.7	2.0
Non-Party	75,038	57,348	36.7	31.2

In Staar, p. 229.
  * Polish United Workers Party [PZPR]
 ** United Peasant Party [ZSL]   (Membership in 1962: 300,000)
*** Democratic Party [SD]   (Membership in 1961: 150,000)

Table 2 — A. National Fronts

Country	Organization	Membership	% of the Electorate
Albania	National Liberation Front (FNC)	645,674	95.0
Bulgaria	National Agrarian Union	120,000	
	Fatherland Front	3,400,000	80-90.0
Czechoslovakia	Slovak National Front	N.A.	60.0
Hungary	Peoples' Patriotic Front	N.A.	60-75.0
Poland	National Front (FN)	N.A.	60.0+
Rumania	People's Democratic Front	N.A.	70-80.0

Table 3 — B. Labor

Country	Organization	Membership
Albania	United Trade Unions of Albania	88,105
Bulgaria	General Workers' Professional Union (ORPS)	1,500,000
Czechoslovakia	Revolutionary Trade Union Movement (ROH)	4,500,000
	Slovak Trade Union Council	
Hungary	National Council of Trade Unions	2,695,000
	National Association of Cooperatives (SZOVOSZ)	1,500,000
Poland	Trade Union Association	6,123,000
Rumania	Central Council of Trade Unions (CCS)	2,706,225

Table 4 — C. Para-Military

Country	Organization	Membership
Albania	Society for Aid to the Army and for Defense (SHNUM)	41,430
Bulgaria	Voluntary Defense Association (DOSO)	250,000
Czechoslovakia	League for Cooperation with the Army (SVAZARM)	N.A.
Hungary	Hungarian Defense Sports Association	N.A.
Poland	League of Soldiers' Friends	N.A.
Rumania	Ready for Work and Defense (GMA)	1,000,000+

Table 5 D. Youth

Country	Organization	Membership
Albania	Working Youth, Union of (Bashkim i Rinise se Punes se Shqiperise)	150,000-200,000
Bulgaria	Dimitrov Communist Youth Union (DKMS), Komsomol Septembriyche or Pioneers, Tchavdartche combined membership	931,692 650,000
Czechoslovakia	Czechoslovak Youth League (CSM) Pioneers "Sparks"	1,518,783
Hungary	Communist Youth League (KISZ) Pioneers	643,500 674,000
Poland	Union of Socialist Youth (ZMS) Union of Peasant Youth (ZMW) Polish Scout Union (ZHP)	615,412 448,000 about 900,000
Rumania	Union of Working Youth (UTM) (Uniunea Tineretului Muncitoresc) Student Union (UAS)	2,100,000

A mass organization rallies its members for a political demonstration in support of the Party and government program.

6 *Economic Development Under Communism*

Table 1 **Index of National Income in Five East European Countries (1950 = 100%)**

Country	Prewar	1949	1950	1952	1954	1956	1958	1960
Bulgaria	81.0	85.0	100.0	121.0	145.0	163.0	196.0	—
Czechoslovakia	82.0	90.0	100.0	119.0	130.0	149.0	173.0	199.0
Hungary	—	82.9	100.0	114.8	124.6	121.0	158.5	186.5
Poland	—	86.9	100.0	114.2	139.4	161.6	186.3	—
Rumania	100.0	—	100.0	137.0	157.0	178.0	214.0	268.0

Source: Martin Hoffmann "How to Read National Income Statistics," **East Europe**, Vol. XI, No. 11, November 1962, p. 12.

134

The Industry and Resources of Communist Eastern Europe

Legend:

- WHEAT
- CORN
- POTATOES
- LIVESTOCK
- AMBER
- FLAX
- ROSES
- PETROLEUM
- COAL
- ALUMINUM
- LIGNITE
- LEAD
- MUNITIONS
- URANIUM
- IRON
- ELECTRIC POWER
- HEAVY INDUSTRY
- LIGHT MANUFACTURING

Table 2   The Share of the Basic Branches of the National Economy in the Formation of the National Income in Percentages

(a) = industry   (b) = agriculture and forestry

		1958	1959	1960	1961
Czechoslovakia	(a)	62.0	65.0	62.0	64.0
	(b)	15.0	13.0	15.0	14.0
Hungary	(a)	49.6	53.7	—	—
	(b)	36.3	24.7	—	—
Poland	(a)	49.0	47.7	48.4	48.4
	(b)	28.2	22.8	23.7	26.1
Rumania	(a)	42.7	42.5	—	45.8
	(b)	34.8	25.1	—	31.1
USSR	(a)	50.2	52.3	52.2	51.8
	(b)	24.1	21.3	20.5	21.2

Table 3   The Annual Increase of the National Income in the Years 1958-1962 in Percentages

	1958	1959	1960	1961	1962
Bulgaria	7.0	21.0	7.0	2.9	—
Czechoslovakia	8.0	6.0	8.0	7.0	0.5
Hungary	6.2	8.0	7.3	5.8	5.0
Poland	5.6	5.3	4.5	8.0	2.5
Rumania	3.4	13.0	10.8	10.9	—
USSR	12.0	8.0	9.0	7.0	6.0

Adam Zwass, "The Economy of the CEMA Countries in 1962," **Zycie Gospodarcze** (Warsaw), March 17, 1963. Figures cited are based on official data of the State Statistical Offices of the countries concerned.

Table 4

Industrial Production of Eastern Europe [1938 + 1962]

Country		STEEL (in 1000 tons)	COAL (in 1000 tons)	OIL (in 1000 tons)	ELECTRICITY (in billion KWH)
Albania	1938	——	3	108	0.009
	1960	——	281	770	0.2
Bulgaria	1938	——	146*	——	0.2
	1962	422	20,800	——	6.0
Czechoslovakia	1938	1,870	15,836	19	4.0
	1962	7,639	92,400	170	28.7
Hungary	1938	640	1,042	43	1.1
	1962	2,300	28,700	1,600	9.1
Poland**	1938	1,890	69,400	141	7.0
	1962	7,700	109,600	1,495	35.4
Rumania	1938	270	299	6,610	1.1
	1962	2,451	10,700	11,864	10.0

*Hard coal only.

**As a result of postwar territorial adjustments (Western Territories) Poland gained approximately 50% additional industrial productive capacity (1938: 100%).

A heavy engineering works in Czechoslovakia

137

Table 5 Agricultural Production of Eastern Europe — Selected Commodities [1938, 1959-61] (in 1000 Tons)

Products	Year	Bulgaria	Czechoslovakia	Hungary	Poland*	Rumania	Albania***	
Wheat	1959	2,437	1,649	1,909	2,484	4,000	121,168	(1957)
	1960	2,389	1,503	1,768	2,303	3,450	96,678	(1958)
	1961	2,034	1,666	1,936	2,792	3,990	101,666	(1959)
	1934-1938**	1,057	1,510	2,220	1,900	2,600	38,570	(1938)
Rye	1959	107	967	443	8,113	128	14,639	(1957)
	1960	82	895	354	7,878	103	8,585	(1958)
	1961	70	994	297	8,356	104	9,089	(1959)
	1938	— no figures available —					3,080	(1938)
Corn	1959	1,506	503	3,558	19	5,580	222,682	(1957)
	1960	1,505	572	3,504	47	5,531	167,481	(1958)
	1961	1,424	461	2,715	33	5,740	208,617	(1959)
	1934-1938**	913	173	2,306	— NFA —	4,032	143,750	(1938)
Barley	1959	560	1,467	1,093	1,043	449	— NFA —	(1959)
	1960	622	1,745	986	1,310	405	— NFA —	(1960)
	1961	612	1,581	984	1,339	468	— NFA —	(1961)
	1938	— no figures available —					— NFA —	(1938)

* As a result of postwar territorial changes Poland lost about 17% of her arable land (1938 = 100%).
** Production figures for this period are averages of the four year period.
*** Figures for Albania are given in full.

Agricultural machinery in use on an East European collective farm.

Table 6 Production of Selected Consumers Goods in Eastern Europe (1962) (in 1000 units)

Countries	Refrigerators	Washing Machines	Televisions	Radios
Bulgaria	N.A.	67.7	15.3	174.6
Czechoslovakia	182.0	N.A.	307.4	289.4
Hungary	17.0	132.0	210.0	258.0
Poland	77.9	580.0	299.9	654.1
Rumania	46.0	76.9	41.4	251.0

Table 7 Per Capita National Income Comparison

Country	Per Capita National Income Annual Avg.** 1957-1959	Rates of Growth of National Income 1959-1960***		
		1958	1959	1960
Bulgaria	200 - 299	6.8	21.6	7.0
Czechoslovakia	700 - 799	8.0	6.0	8.8
Hungary	500 - 599	6.0	7.0	5-6.0
Poland	400 - 499	5.4	5.6	5.0
Rumania	200 - 299	3.4	13.1	8.0

**In US dollars.
Source: **US Economic Almanac**, 1962, pp. 490ff.
***Percentage increases from previous year.
Source: **UN Economic Survey of Europe**, 1960, p. 8, Chapter II.

An East European truck
repair shop.

Table 8 Average Export Wheat Prices Received by the Soviet Union

	1959		1960		1961	
	Average Price① Per Ton	% of Soviet Average Price	Average Price② Per Ton	% of Soviet Average Price	Average Price Per Ton	% of Soviet Average Price
Soviet Union③	285.41	100.0	62.77	100.0	61.83	100.0
IMPORTERS						
Albania	314.92	110.3	68.22	108.7	66.01	106.8
Bulgaria	334.27	117.1	74.83	119.2	71.06	114.9
Czechoslovakia	294.41	103.2	66.78	106.4	67.61	109.3
Hungary	315.72	110.6	65.83	104.9	65.86	106.5
Poland	302.94	106.1	64.04	102.0	62.48	101.1
Rumania	—	—	73.98	117.9	—	—
England	234.99	82.3	53.28	85.1	54.15	87.6
France	251.17	80.0	—	—	57.16	92.4
Italy	—	—	55.42	88.3	55.31	89.3
Sweden	256.98	90.0	58.33	92.9	58.53	94.7
West Germany	234.02	82.0	53.80	85.7	55.36	89.5

Source: Foreign Trade of the USSR for 1959, Moscow 1960.
Source: Foreign Trade of the USSR for 1961, Moscow 1962.
① Average prices per ton in old rubles for 1959 [f.o:b. Export Port of the Soviet Union, or RR Station at the Soviet border]
② In new rubles (4.4444 old rubles equal 1 new ruble)
③ Average prices received by the Soviet Union based on old Soviet exports including countries importing small quantities from the USSR.

Table 9 Proportion of the Trade Turnover of CEMA Nations with Other CMEA Nations① (in percentage)

Year	Bulgaria	Czechoslovakia	Hungary	Poland	Rumania	USSR
1938	30	19	23	13	25	7
1956	77	59	54	57	72	50
1960	79	64	62	57	67	49

Table 10 Proportion of the Trade Turnover of CEMA Nations with the USSR② (in percentage)

Year	Bulgaria	Czechoslovakia	Hungary	Poland	Rumania	Average
1938	0	3	0	1	0	2
1956	47	32	24	31	48	36
1960	N.A.	34	30	30	40	36

① Frederic L. Pryor, The Communist Foreign Trade System, The M.I.T. Press, 1963, p. 165
② IBID, p. 187

(7) Elements of Cohesion

The Communist Information Bureau (COMINFORM) 1947-1956.

The Information Bureau of the Communist Parties (COMINFORM) was established on October 5, 1947, following a meeting of the Communist Parties of Bulgaria, Czechoslovakia, France, Hungary, Italy, Poland, Rumania, the USSR and Yugoslavia held between September 22-27, 1947, at Szklarska Poreba [a resort town in Southwestern Poland]. The purpose of the meeting was to re-establish an institutional framework for a closer association of Communist Parties which had been disrupted by the dissolution of the Communist International (COMINTERN) on May 15, 1943. According to A. A. Zhdanov, the spokesman for the Soviet delegation "... the present position of the Communist Parties has its shortcomings. Some comrades understood the dissolution of the COMINTERN to imply the elimination of all ties, of all contact between the fraternal Communist Parties. But experience has shown that such mutual isolation of the Communist Parties is wrong, harmful, and in fact unnatural."*

*Quoted in ZKB, Soviet Bloc, p. 60. (1960 Ed)

This thesis was supported by all present, with the exception of Gomulka who expressed reservations about the usefulness of such a supra-national organization of Communist Parties. Conversely, the would-be revisionist Yugoslavs endorsed the Soviet position in very strong terms, stressing the genuine orthodoxy and the close adherence of the Yugoslav Party line to the policies of the Soviet leadership.

The next meeting of the Cominform gathered on June 28, 1948, for the purpose of expelling the recalcitrant Yugoslavs and to reassert the monolithic ideological unity of the "purified" international Communist movement. The organization's headquarters and the editorial offices of its weekly "FOR LASTING PEACE, FOR PEOPLE'S DEMOCRACY" were transferred from Belgrade to Bucharest. From the start, it was apparent that the Cominform was to be a worthy heir to its predecessor, the Comintern: the Bucharest center employed 1200-1800 specialists in five departments, published its weekly newspaper in several languages, and was run by P. F. Yudin, an erudite representative of the Soviet Secret Police.

Elaborate organization and propaganda activities notwithstanding, the Cominform could not undermine or destroy the Yugoslav heretics and soon after its fourth and last plenary session in the fall of 1949 waned into semi-oblivion. Since Stalin preferred to deal with foreign Communists strictly on a bilateral basis, and the Chinese Party either decided not to join or was kept out, there was little need for pretensions to internationalism during Stalin's lifetime. Khrushchev, in his turn, was not enthusiastic about the Cominform since its very history was so closely linked with the anti-Yugoslav campaign and the attendant purges of East European Communists. After the Soviet-Yugoslav reconciliation in 1955 and certainly after the Twentieth Soviet Party Congress it was a foregone conclusion that the Cominform had to go. It was declared dissolved on April 17, 1956.

If there ever were any plans to reconstitute the discredited organization, these were forcefully disclaimed in Soviet declarations during and following October 1956. In 1957, Khrushchev, having disposed of the anti-Party group that represented the greatest single obstacle to the realignment of the "fraternal Communist Parties" on non-Stalinist terms, invited the leaders of the ruling Parties to take part in the 40th anniversary celebration of the October Revolution. From a series of conferences on that occasion there emerged a new formula for cooperation on the basis of a "Socialist Commonwealth" which implied a workable compromise between those seeking greater freedom for their respective parties and those who pleaded for a return to a modified Stalinist, strongly centralized pattern of interparty relations.

The premises of the 1957 Moscow Declaration, however, did not prove viable. During the next four years polycentrism manifested itself in Gomulka's "Polish Road to Socialism," Tito's "Yugoslav Road," Chairman Mao's "Great Leap to Communism," and in Hoxha's steadfast loyalty to Stalinist policies. The 1961 Declaration of Eighty-one Communist Parties, though the product of hard bargaining and ostensibly representing the consensus of the world Communist movement, was but a stop-gap measure to prevent an open split between the Soviet and Chinese Parties. It was the hour of truth for the East European Parties as well; a clear choice had to be made between the views of the two strongest parties. Hoxha opted for Mao and the rest of Communist Eastern Europe chose to align themselves with the Russians.

This new equilibrium of Communist forces required new institutional arrangements to match the changed circumstances. Instead of a central international Communist organization, it is now the International Department for Ruling Parties of the Soviet Party Secretariat that maintains communication with its counterparts in other Parties. Since 1958 a new monthly journal "World Marxist Review" is published in Prague, offering reports by Communists from Iceland to Capetown, but no orders from Chairman Khrushchev. Finally, the East European Communist leaders now meet their Soviet counterparts to discuss matters of mutual interest, and to formulate policies for the Soviet bloc.

Table 1 **Cominform (1947-1956)***

Executive Council
16 members
2 representatives for each Party

Departments
Military Department
- foreign policy
- trade unions
- youth
- religious questions

Political Department
- recruiting for the formation of international brigades
- intelligence
- transport
- armaments
- communications
- operations

Economic Department
- central accounting bureau
- CEMA affairs

Propaganda Department
- world revolution
  - Slav
  - German-Scandinavian
  - Anglo-Saxon
  - Latin
  - Colonial Countries
- internal affairs

Information Department (publications)

Cadres Section
directly under Executive Council

*After the failure of the anti-Yugoslav campaign, some departments and sections were probably disbanded or transferred to Moscow and there incorporated into various Party and government organizations.

143

The Council for Economic Mutual Assistance (CEMA)

CEMA was founded in Moscow on January 21, 1949, by Bulgaria, Czechoslovakia, Hungary, Poland, Rumania and the USSR. Albania joined in February 1949 and East Germany in September 1950. After 1955, the Far Eastern Communist states sent observers to the organization's more important meetings.

The group's original purpose was to counteract, largely in a propagandistic sense, the impact of the Marshall Plan, to further the expansion of intra-bloc trade by boosting exchanges of raw materials, food-stuffs and industrial goods, and to integrate the development programs of the newly formed Soviet orbit in Eastern Europe.

However, local interpretations of Stalin's economic dogmas encouraged the formulation of separate, uncoordinated economic plans in the CEMA countries which emphasized autarchic principles, made for considerable duplication of effort, and fostered national economic rivalries.

Although there were some attempts to give vitality to this largely still-born organization during the years 1953 to 1955, they did not bear fruit until 1956. In that year the Council created several Standing Commissions to make recommendations on measures to bring about production coordination, specialization and standardization, and also to serve as a clearing house for the exchange of technological and scientific information. The latter remained the Council's most important function until 1959 when, at the Twenty-first Soviet Party Congress, Premier Khrushchev called for a concerted effort to increase economic cooperation between the Soviet Union and the East European members of the bloc.

The road toward this goal has not been easy or smooth. Albania was ousted from the group in 1962 for political and ideological reasons. Economic nationalism has manifested itself in Polish and Rumanian demands for increased trade with the West. The disparity in levels of economic development between such countries as Czechoslovakia and Bulgaria has not been significantly narrowed. Nevertheless, the Council has made remarkable progress toward closer economic integration despite the persistence of many bilateral links between individual countries.

The Friendship Oil Pipeline now connects the USSR with Poland, East Germany, Czechoslovakia and Hungary and it is later expected to extend into Rumania and Bulgaria. The United Power System, whose administrative headquarters are in Prague, is very largely completed and connects the power grids of all the East European states with the Soviet Ukraine. Eventually it is to link up with the generating facilities of Siberia.

Some progress is also being made in fostering multilateral long term capital investment and in the synchronization of economic plans, not only in the current phase ending in 1965, but as far into the future as 1980.

Significantly, the effect of these various endeavors has not only been to increase efficiency in certain areas of production and to boost trade turnover between CEMA members. The proliferating,

CEMA-inspired economic ties have subtly bound the East European countries closer to the USSR and given the latter a degree of control on the economic plane which acts as a significant counterweight to the increased freedom which has had to be conceded to them in the political area.

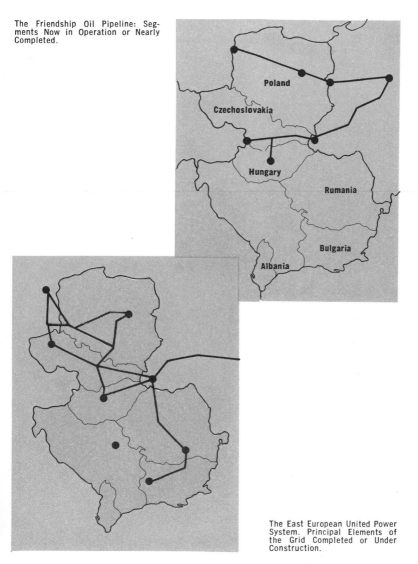

The Friendship Oil Pipeline: Segments Now in Operation or Nearly Completed.

The East European United Power System. Principal Elements of the Grid Completed or Under Construction.

Table 2 CEMA ORGANIZATION

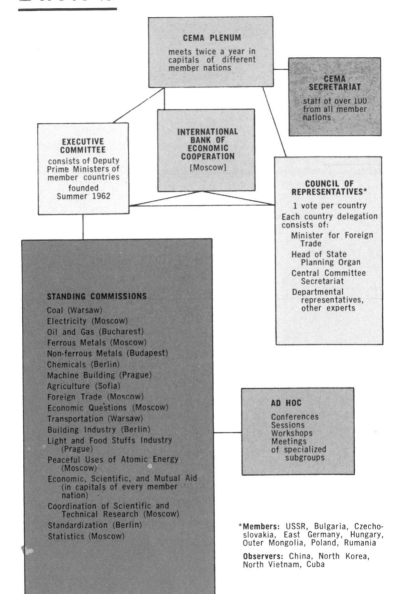

CEMA PLENUM

meets twice a year in capitals of different member nations

CEMA SECRETARIAT

staff of over 100 from all member nations

EXECUTIVE COMMITTEE

consists of Deputy Prime Ministers of member countries
founded Summer 1962

INTERNATIONAL BANK OF ECONOMIC COOPERATION
[Moscow]

COUNCIL OF REPRESENTATIVES*

1 vote per country
Each country delegation consists of:
Minister for Foreign Trade
Head of State Planning Organ
Central Committee Secretariat
Departmental representatives, other experts

STANDING COMMISSIONS

Coal (Warsaw)
Electricity (Moscow)
Oil and Gas (Bucharest)
Ferrous Metals (Moscow)
Non-ferrous Metals (Budapest)
Chemicals (Berlin)
Machine Building (Prague)
Agriculture (Sofia)
Foreign Trade (Moscow)
Economic Questions (Moscow)
Transportation (Warsaw)
Building Industry (Berlin)
Light and Food Stuffs Industry (Prague)
Peaceful Uses of Atomic Energy (Moscow)
Economic, Scientific, and Mutual Aid (in capitals of every member nation)
Coordination of Scientific and Technical Research (Moscow)
Standardization (Berlin)
Statistics (Moscow)

AD HOC

Conferences
Sessions
Workshops
Meetings
of specialized subgroups

***Members:** USSR, Bulgaria, Czecho-slovakia, East Germany, Hungary, Outer Mongolia, Poland, Rumania

Observers: China, North Korea, North Vietnam, Cuba

The Warsaw Pact
Treaty of Friendship, Cooperation, and Mutual Assistance
| signed in Warsaw, May 14, 1955 |

Concluded in response to ratification of the Paris Accords and West German entry into NATO, as well as to legalize the presence of Soviet troops in Rumania and Hungary after the conclusion of the Austrian State Treaty in 1955, the Pact supplemented but did not supersede the postwar bilateral treaties between the USSR and the other founding members: Albania, Bulgaria, Czechoslovakia, Hungary, Poland, Rumania and East Germany.

The treaty's main provision calls for mutual assistance in the event of an attack from outside. The member nations also pledged "to refrain in their international relations from the threat or use of force ..." in settling their international disputes.

There were two noteworthy aspects of the Pact. Membership was declared open to all nations regardless of their political sympathies and East German manpower contributions to the organization were not to be made effective until a later date. While the former was a purely declarative statement of propaganda character, the latter was clearly a concession to Polish and Czech sensitivities concerning the revival of an armed Germany.

In order to restore the shaken prestige of the Soviet Army after the events in Poland and the revolt in Hungary during 1956 and 1957, a supplementary series of bilateral treaties were concluded between the USSR and Poland, East Germany, Hungary and Rumania providing for the continued presence of Soviet troops in those countries. Although the Pact envisaged a unified command of the armed forces of its members, this has not been implemented. So far Soviet Marshals Konev and Grechko have served as Commanders-in-Chief, presiding over the still un-integrated national armies. It was only in 1962 that the first regional military exercises of international character were held. In the fall of 1963 Polish, Czech, East German and Soviet troops took part in joint military exercises. However, it appears that nuclear weapons commands have not been integrated and are manned solely by Soviet personnel.

The most important central body of the Pact is its Political Consultative Committee with a permanent Secretariat and a permanent Sub-Committee on International Affairs. Four or five meetings of the first were known to have been held until 1963. The last meeting was attended by the Party leaders of the respective countries and was primarily concerned with the nuclear test ban treaty negotiations.

China, North Korea, North Viet Nam and Outer Mongolia were represented by observers at the meetings of the Political Consultative Committee. As far as it is known, China, Albania and North Korea did not participate in the Committee's latest session.

147

Table 3
Military Strength of Eastern Europe (1960)

Albania	21,000 men
Bulgaria	100,000 "
Czechoslovakia	150,000 "
East Germany	65,000 "
Hungary	75,000 "
Poland	200,000 "
Rumania	200,000 "

Air forces: 2,900 planes [80 per cent jet fighters]

The seven countries can mobilize 60 divisions with 800,000 men plus 400,000 in para-military formations.

Source: **Revue Militaire Générale** (Paris), January 1961

 # Writers and Writing Under Communism

1. An Introductory Essay on East European Writers
2. Writers and Writing
   a. Bulgaria
   b. Czechoslovakia
   c. Hungary
   d. Poland
   e. Rumania
3. Bibliography of recently published works of fiction and non-fiction from Eastern Europe in English

East European Writers

The intellectuals of Eastern Europe have been called the keepers of their countries' conscience. Men of letters have earned and preserved this reputation by being the spokesmen for their nations, and representing the peoples' traditional distrust of politicians. History has shown that this sense of mission was real and not a pretension of a handful of intellectuals in the largely uneducated societies of the area. The national, cultural, and political awakening in the 19th century Rumania, Hungary, Bohemia, and Poland would not have been possible without the efforts of historians, writers, poets, philosophers, and journalists who fought domestic and foreign oppressors and at the same time educated their people.

These time-honored traditions, though sometimes suppressed, and at other times merely tolerated by the authorities, survived the Second World War and were kept alive under Communism by East Europe's "natural elite" — its writers and intellectuals.

Soon after the Communist takeover, however, it became painfully clear that the Communist Parties were unwilling to tolerate the activities of any potential competitors for the allegiance of the masses. Writers, the traditional dissenters, capable of negating much of the Communist indoctrination efforts, thus became one of the chief targets of Communist hostility. Everywhere in the area, the Parties introduced a new yardstick of artistic achievement — socialist realism. The term was said to have been first coined by Maxim Gorky, but became known after the war through the writings of Andrej Zhdanov, a Secretary of the Soviet Communist Party in charge of literature and ideology. Socialist realism remains a rather elusive term. It is supposed to represent a translation of the Party policies into the language of literature and art. It is to be "socialist" by reflecting "the problems of society in the epoch of building socialism," and it is to be "realist" by describing life not only as it is, but as it *should* be, according to the "political and ideological consciousness" of the artist. This "consciousness," in turn, should be a militant, yet artistic, reassertion and advocacy of the Party's current line.

The total suppression of non-Communist literature was achieved in Eastern Europe by 1949. The cost of imposing alien, dogmatic standards of literature and art was high and led to the degeneration of artistic excellence and the intellectual debasement of its individual practitioners.

Zhdanovism in literature required a high degree of flexibility, constant compromises with one's conscience, and rejection of the "non-progressive" features of the nation's heritage. It demanded uncritical flattery of the achievements of Soviet "socialist" literature, and the prostitution of one's own talents when producing poems, novels, and plays on demand from the local Parties.

Through its monopoly of newspapers, journals, and publishing houses, the Party could effectively silence those who did not comply. Nor were Communist efforts to eradicate internal dissent confined to writers and artists: after 1949 thousands of intellectuals were subjected to demotion, internment or deportation.

These repressive measures, however, did not involve the younger intellectual members of the "new class," youthful writers of working class or peasant origin or even alienated offspring of the middle class. By and large, these remained unscathed during the Stalinist literary purges. Nor had they any reason to set their pens against the "collective wisdom" of the Party. Its teachings filled their intellectual horizon and comfortably dispelled any doubts concerning the correctness of Stalinist policies. Many young intellectuals sincerely believed that political repression, economic deprivations and purges were inevitable but transitory phenomena to be followed by an era of the "new man" and the emergence of a Communist ethic sustained by

149

a classless society that enforces its moral code through comradely persuasion rather than police methods.

However, as the post-Stalin thaw progressed, many young Communists suddenly realized that Stalinism had entailed not only economic hardships and human deprivations, but a moral corruption

DE-STALINIZATION

of public life by a bureaucratized and callous ruling Communist Party. Wiktor Woroszylski writes in *Notes for a Biography:*

> ... the more the exposure of errors, degeneracies and plain crimes proceeded — responsibility for which rests not only on their direct inspirers and executors but also on those who feared to oppose them, or who acted out of ignorance or blindness — the more difficult did it become to endure one's soul searching and breast-beating. A few years earlier I had put part of my heart into a poem about the alleged treason of Yugoslavia. How could I feel otherwise than cheated now that I learned that this too had been a provocation? [published in March, 1956]

Few events in modern intellectual history can be compared to the protest movement engendered by the "thaw" and the revelations in Khrushchev's Secret Speech. The revolt was a new era in East European literature. The Stalinist hegemony in cultural life was repudiated and a beginning was made in the reconquest of literature by those to whom it rightly belongs: the writers of East Europe.

Bulgarian Writing

The Bulgarian literary ferment began in 1955 with what was officially called "bourgeois manifestations among writers." In the Spring of 1956 a group of writers, Emil Manov, Todor Genov, Lyuben Stanev, Stoyan Dashkalov, all of whom were Party members except

Stanev, launched a drive calling for an extraordinary Party Congress to carry out the resolution of the earlier 20th Soviet Party Congress. They also denied the Party's right to control the arts and to impose socialist realism as the only yardstick of artistic merit.

Since the Bulgarian Party could not repudiate the Soviet initiative, it decided to temporize by granting some concessions to the most outspoken intellectuals and to permit the appearance of the dissident literary periodical *Plamuk* in 1957.

The historical and cultural affinity of Bulgarian and Russian literature caused the former to take its cues from current Soviet literary debates, rather than from the West, as was the case elsewhere in Eastern Europe.

Nevertheless Bulgarian writers were still accused of "misrepresenting the errors caused by the cult of personality," which many countered with a "strike of silence."

The Party indeed found it necessary to restate its views on the literary situation:

> Everybody is free to write and say what he pleases ... however ... the Party is free to expel members who use the Party label to preach anti-Party views.... The borderline between what is pro-Party and what is anti-Party, will be determined by the Party program, by the tactical Party resolutions, and Party statutes....This is how things will be in our Party, gentlemen ...

It added that "... a writer does not have to be a Communist, but his position must coincide with the Party position. Party-mindedness is obligatory for Party and non-Party members alike."

There ensued something of a stalemate between the authorities and the Bulgarian literary community as the government continued to feud with Yugoslavia and to pursue its own, ill-fated equivalent of the Chinese "Great Leap Forward." Both drives, however, resulted in failure as did official attempts to curb the influence of Western ideas.

At present, therefore, most Bulgarian writers are engaged in genuine literary pursuits once more. They have discarded the "positive heroes" demanded by "socialist realism" and deal instead with themes of love, friendship, conscience and human sorrow.

Czechoslovak Writing

In Czechoslovakia the "thaw" also gathered momentum in 1955. In the months following the Geneva summit conference, a somewhat freer expression of views concerning the worst abuses of the Stalinist past began in literary magazines.

The President of the Republic, Antonin Zapotocky, tried at first to defend literary orthodoxy by warning that:

> Many of our artists are suffering from bellyache. They wish us well and are for socialism ... but they say: give us complete artistic freedom! My answer is: we shall not give artists that sort of freedom because we shall never succeed in building socialism in that way.

Nevertheless the Czech Writers' Congress of April 1956, turned into something of a demonstration demanding that:

a) imprisoned authors be released;
b) literature be freed of censorship and Party guidance;
c) writers be permitted once again to follow their conscience.

Although none of these demands were granted, ideological controls were slightly relaxed and new literary periodicals helped the revival of poetry and literary criticism.

There was, however, nothing like a sincere official commitment to liberalization. The Party purposefully sabotaged and delayed the publication of manuscripts submitted after April 1956 and it was thus not until 1958 that there was any evidence of improved literary standards. Three works of the period are notable; each had flesh and blood heroes and each earned the Party's scorn and suspicion. These were: *Follow the Green Light* by Eduard Valenta, *Frontier Town* by Karel Ptacnik, and *Cowards*, by Josef Skvorecky.

Nevertheless, in 1959 Stalinism in Czechoslovak literature had not been seriously shaken. In an effort to strengthen the forces of orthodoxy, Ladislav Stoll, the one-time Zhdanovite Minister of Culture, formed a "Committee for Socialist Culture." This experiment was a dismal failure because the majority of writers simply boycotted the organization and went on undermining past policies and institutions. Neither the Socialist Constitution of 1960 nor the Party's conciliatory gestures after the 22nd Soviet Party Congress, did much to impress either Czech or Slovakian writers.

The much delayed change in climate came in December 1962, and it was April 1963 before the Slovak Writers' Congress convened where formerly imprisoned Communist writers such as Laco Novomesky and Eduard Goldstücker were permitted to speak of Stalinist mistakes in literature. President Novotny, who attended the Congress, was strongly attacked by several young Communist writers for the slowness with which de-Stalinization was proceeding.

By the end of 1963, it was perfectly evident that the majority of both Czech and Slovak writers had declared in favor of more energetic liberalization and that their hand was substantially stronger in negotiations with the Party hierarchy than it had been when they had first attempted to assert their claims in 1956. Thus, though it has been slow in coming, there is now much evidence to suggest that intellectual ferment and artistic experimentation are likely to maintain and increase their momentum.

Hungarian Writing

When Imre Nagy was made Premier and launched the New Course in June 1953 several young Communist writers suddenly came to see the harsh realities of life and began to appreciate the full extent of moral and material damage which Rakosi's ruthless Stalinism had caused. Non-Communist writers, often victims of administrative measures imposed upon Hungary's cultural life by Jozsef Revai, Politburo member in charge of literature and arts, needed no official revelations to know the truth about the country's conditions.

Communist writers and their elder colleagues now found themselves in full agreement as to the need for supporting Nagy's measures of political and economic liberalization.

The literary products of this tacit understanding generally

consisted of articles and studies in the best traditions of the crusading muckraker type Populist Hungarian literature of the thirties. Just as a generation before, when groups of young sociologists, students and journalists descended on the countryside to investigate the dismal conditions of the rural poor, and published their findings, sharply critical of the authoritarian Horthy regime, the new village explorers visited starving collective farmers, neglected industrial and mining settlements and brought back stories of misery and despair. They also showed the darker reality behind the poverty — that of the prisons, unmarked graves, unclaimed bodies, false accusers and tortured men and women. It was significant that the most outspoken and embittered testimonies came from Communists: Lajos Konya, Peter Kuczka, Laszlo Benjamin and Karoly Jobbagy.

In 1955, when Rakosi returned to power, a rebellion against the Party took form under the leadership of Gyula Hay and Tibor Dery, both long-time Communists. A March 1955 resolution of the Party severely attacked "the bourgeois revisionist" trend developing among writers, but the dissidents refused to capitulate. At the Writers' Union meeting in November 1955 a group of Communist authors threatened to leave their Union posts and drafted a memorandum to the Party Central Committee. The memorandum was signed by 53 outstanding writers and artists whose defiance increased still further after Khrushchev's denunciation of Stalin when they began demanding Rakosi's removal from leadership.

By the Spring of 1956 the writers' attack against Stalinist policies and against Rakosi's group in particular broadened into a concerted effort by Communists and non-Communists alike. At the insistence of young writers the subject of Laszlo Nemeth's play "Galileo," Tibor Dery's censored novel, "The Answer" and Gyorgy Lukacs' condemned works on Marxist philosophy came to the forefront of discussion and developed into objects of a running battle between the Writers' Union weekly *Irodalmi Ujsay* and *Szabad Nep*, the Party daily.

Debates in literary journals and at the Petofi Circle came to involve many students, artists, and Party members who previously might have been disinterested in literary politics. Rakosi's timely fall in July 1956 prevented him from carrying out a plan to purge no less than four hundred writers and intellectuals. The September session of the Writers' Association voted the Stalinists out of power and installed a new leadership that included the outstanding Hungarian men of letters, Party and non-Party alike.

During the Revolution the writers remained firm supporters of the Nagy government. A group of former Populists and writers of peasant origin went so far as to form an eleven-member supervisory board of the Petofi Party to replace the radical Peasant Party disbanded by the Communists in 1947.

After the Soviet Army crushed the Revolution, the writers had only one weapon of resistance left to them, that of collective silence. The Party was faced with an embarrassing literary void. To fill it, several minor talents were brought to the fore and entrusted with the task of "unmasking the imperialist instigated Fascist counter-revolution." Since, however, this "unmasking" did not make for digestable reading, Hungarian and Western classics had to be reissued.

Neither the Party's July 1957 theses on literature nor the ensuing anti-revisionist campaign did much to induce first rate writers to publish. Many Communist writers, including Dery, Hay, Konya, Benjamin and Kuczka were imprisoned; four of Imre Nagy's journalist friends had been executed, and the non-Communists remained unwilling to recant their "cosmopolitan nationalism." This stalemate lasted until 1960 when some of the rebellious writers were driven by sheer lack of funds to go through the motions of an unconvincing self-criticism and resumed their literary activities.

In 1961 several imprisoned Communist writers were set free, thus marking the return of Dery, Hay, Benjamin and Kuczka to the literary scene. The first published writings of these men betrayed remarkably few effects of prison life. On the contrary, Dery's new novels, Benjamin's new poems and Nemeth's plays showed a measured approval of the achievements of the Kadar government in relaxing most of the unseemly features of censorship and permitting a wide latitude for literary criticism of the system's shortcomings. Next to the older generation a number of sadder and wiser young writers have appeared on the literary scene in recent years. Their works, although clearly reflecting attitudes of reconciliation with the existing political limitations on artistic freedom, follow national and Western traditions and show few signs of socialist realist orthodoxy.

Polish Writing

The age of Stalinism began in Poland in 1948. Political controls cut off the country's writers from their Western colleagues. However, due to the Polish Party's particular historical background no blood was shed during the Stalinist period and the victims of political trials and thousands of arrested men and women were allowed to live eventually to witness the victorious Polish October. Although few if any writers were touched by the purges, the expected consequences of open literary deviation were no secret to Polish intellectuals.

Thus, even in the "dark ages" of 1949-55 it was possible for Polish intellectual life to survive. In spite of Czeslaw Milosz' fears, the minds of Polish writers and philosophers were not "captivated" by the Party, for there was enough laxity and inefficiency of control to allow some hope for an eventual change.

Special circumstances notwithstanding, Stalinism was real enough in Poland. Recalling these times, Pawel Hertz described the premises of the "cultural vanguard" Writers' Union as *The House of the Dead* — not of dead men but of intellectually and morally deceased literary officials.

The Polish literary "thaw" was heralded by a poem written by the long-time Communist, Adam Wazyk. The *Poem for Adults* was published in August 1955. Wazyk not only refused to accept the Polish reality but condemned it. Drabness, hopelessness, and emptiness of life were sharply contrasted with the Party's glowing promises. The former believer had turned emotionally barren. He simply could not take it any more and had audaciously crossed the borderline of permissible criticism.

The Party's reply came swiftly: "How does it happen that a Party poet in our country writes about our life in a poem full of bitter disillusionment, if not outright contempt.... Wazyk indulges in a cold position of generalization in such a way that he could expose himself to the accusation of irresponsibility.... This poem is bad and cruel half-truth ..."

The first months of 1956 witnessed a growing protest movement of writers and journalists demanding a thoroughgoing de-Stalinization of public life. Following the Poznan riots of June 1956, these men, openly defiant of official interpretations of the event, came to the aid of the arrested demonstrators and echoed their demands in newspapers and literary journals.

In October, the writers threw their full support behind Gomulka and his program. After the failure of the Hungarian revolution, members of the Polish Writers' Union who had been in Budapest publicly contradicted Soviet allegations concerning the nature of the uprising. The Hungarian experience had shown what could have happened in Poland without the firm alliance of Party, intellectuals, and the entire people which kept Russian tanks out of Warsaw in the crucial October days.

After October 1956 there was a flowering of creative energies, lasting until September 1957, when it began to recede slowly under official pressure. During this time an amazing variety of protest literature appeared ranging from the learned philosophical disquisitions of Leszek Kolakowski to the biting satires of Marek Hlasko.

In *The Responsibility and History* (published in four installments in the periodical *Nowa Kultura* in September 1957) Kolakowski's criticism is not directed at specific actions of the Party but to some of the essential premises underlying Party actions and its claims to ideological hegemony over its members and society at large. He attacks historical determinism, and lauds individual morality as superior to collective morality. Kolakowski accepts the goal of socialism but refuses to support it on Communist terms.

In *Transitory and Permanent Aspects of Marxism,* Kolakowski demanded a thorough re-examination of the Marxist heritage, with particular attention to Stalin's vulgarizing influences and neo-Stalinist attempts to reintroduce dogmatism as a valid ideological posture in philosophical debates. This attitude was expressed again in another Kolakowski piece, *The Priest and the Jester,* where he says concisely: "We declare ourselves in favor of the philosophy of the jester, namely the attitude of negative vigilance in the face of any kind of absolute."

Jerzy Andrzejewski's *The Inquisitors* is an exposé of the totalitarianism of a bygone age. Police methods have changed little during the last four hundred years, and the evils engendered by fanatic beliefs have remained the same. Chief Inquisitor Torquemada is explicit in explaining the foundations of his power: "... it is based on universal fear ... with the exception of a few who obey freely everybody must be so afraid that no one is capable of even imagining an existence free of fear."

But the Polish writers of 1957 feared no more: Andrzejewski was among the six eminent Polish literary figures, including Adam Wazyk, who turned in their Party cards in protest against the reimposition of censorship by Gomulka.

By the end of 1957, there had appeared a note of pessimism in the writings of nearly all major and lesser Polish writers and poets.

The Intellectuals of Eastern Europe: Some Polish and Hungarian Portraits

TADEUSZ ROZEWICZ

GYULA ILLYES

MAREK HLASKO

JAROSLAW IWASZKIEWICZ

GYORGY LUKACS

TIBOR DERY

SLAWOMIR MROZEK

Disappointment with the results of October 1956 led to a return to prudence, which manifested itself by a slow retreat from the earlier and exuberant Western orientation and by a renewed appreciation of Russia's power in Polish affairs. The writers seemed to recognize the simple truth that no one from the outside would or could come to rescue the Polish intellectuals.

In mid-December 1958 at the Writers' Congress in Wroclaw, an open rift developed between the writers and regime spokesmen over cultural policies and censorship. A year later the Party moved to "rectify the abnormality of the situation in the recent period." Since then Gomulka has disbanded such centers of dissent as the Crooked Circle Club, dismissed several liberal editors of literary journals, reintroduced relatively stringent standards of censorship and required ideological purity of Polish cultural workers.

The Polish United Workers Party plenum on ideology and culture held in July 1963 signaled a return to even greater stringency: its sharply worded resolution was critical of Western influences and demanded the promotion of a partisan spirit in works of literature and art.

The end, however, is not in sight. As the Polish students say, "thinking has a colossal future ..." And so does Polish art and literature which, despite setbacks and unfulfilled expectations, has not lost its vitality.

Rumanian Writing

It would be difficult, if not impossible, to detect in Rumania signs of meaningful and open literary opposition to the Party before 1958. In 1956 one isolated author, Alexandru Jar, uttered some critical remarks and was promptly expelled from the Party for "vile slanders and insinuations."

Rumanian intellectuals, however, were prompted by post-1956 Polish and Hungarian literary activity to attempt to deviate from the rules of socialist realism and to indulge in subtle revisions of literary forms in defiance of the Party's inflexible ideological stand on literary matters.

This trend was met by an official attack on the "ideologically defective," "bourgeois-cosmopolitan," apolitical, and escapist works of several Rumanian writers. During the subsequent campaign, several writers went through the ritual of self-criticism and promised to conform again to "Leninist principles." The outcome, however, seems to have been indecisive and a stalemate persisted until 1962 when Mihail Beniuc, the head of the Writers' Union, made some conciliatory gestures toward previously condemned authors and promised to implement the more relaxed policies enunciated at the 22nd Soviet Party Congress. Recently, as Rumania adopted a somewhat independent stand on economic and political matters, there were also signs of further relaxation of political control over literature. Nationalist sentiment appears to be on the rise, possibly because of tacit cooperation between the Party and the writers to enhance Rumania's stature within the Soviet bloc.

Bibliography of Recently Published Works of Fiction and Non-Fiction from Eastern Europe in English Translation

ACZEL, Tamas and Tibor Meray, *The Revolt of the Mind,* New York: Praeger, 1959

ANDRZEJEWSKI, Jerzy, *The Inquisitors,* New York: Knopf, 1960
Sons and Comrades, London: Allen & Unwin, 1960

DERY, Tibor, *Niki,* New York: Doubleday, 1958

DUMITRU, Petru, *Family Jewels,* New York: Pantheon, 1961

HLASKO, Marek, *The Eighth Day of the Week,* New York: Dutton, 1958
Next Stop — Paradise, New York: Dutton, 1960

JUHASZ, William and Abraham Rothberg, editors,
Flashes in the Night: A Collection of Stories from Contemporary Hungary, New York: Random House, 1958

KUNCEWICZ, Maria, ed., *The Modern Polish Mind.* An Anthology. New York: Little, Brown and Co., 1962

MANNING, Clarence A. and Roman Smal-Stocki,
The History of Modern Bulgarian Literature. New York: Bookman Assoc., 1960

MAYEWSKI, Pawel, ed., *The Broken Mirror*:
A Collection of Writings from Contemporary Poland.
New York: Random House, 1958

ORDON, Edmund, ed., *Ten Contemporary Polish Stories,* Wayne University Press, 1958

PALACZI-HORVATH, George, *The Undefeated,* Boston: Atlantic-Little, Brown, 1959

ed., *One Sentence on Tyranny.*
Hungarian Literary Gazette Anthology, London:
The Waverley Press, 1957

STILLMAN, Edmund, ed., *Bitter Harvest,* New York: Praeger, 1959

SZABO, Magda, *The Fawn,* New York: Knopf, 1963

A Selective List of Communist Terms

APPARATCHIK: A full-time, paid functionary of a Communist Party organization.

COLLECTIVE LEADERSHIP: A term used by Stalin's heirs denoting their intention to return to 'Leninist norms of Party life' and to effect a sharp break with the dictatorial one-man rule practiced by Joseph Stalin.

CULT OF PERSONALITY: The practice of attributing exceptional human, intellectual and political qualities to a leader in a Communist state. The concept is uniquely associated with the autocratic behavior of Stalin and certain East European Communist leaders who attained power under his aegis.

DEVIATION: A real or alleged departure from ideological orthodoxy as interpreted at any given time by the Communist Party leadership.

DOGMATISTS: Holders of the notion that the teachings of Marx and Lenin must be literally and rigidly interpreted and seen as imutable truths. A term generally applied to the most intransigent and belligerent among Communists who cherish the classical belief in class war and the inevitability of conflict between Communist and non-Communist societies.

FACTIONALISM: The activity of an actual or potential group within a Communist Party which would seek to oppose the policies endorsed by a majority of the leadership.

NATIONAL COMMUNISM: The belief of some Communist leaders — notably Tito, Nagy, Gomulka — that the world Communist movement need not and should not, on all matters, be centrally controlled by the leadership of the Communist Party of the Soviet Union; the view that different states and peoples can proceed toward a common Communist goal at different rates of speed and by taking into account local conditions and potentialities.

NEO-STALINISM: A term currently associated with the political practices and beliefs of Communists seeking a return to the totalitarian policies and methods employed by Stalin during his long years of one-man rule.

NEW COURSE: A two year period immediately following Stalin's death in 1953 during which the stringent economic policies which were introduced with the Communist take-over of Eastern Europe were slightly relaxed and an effort was made to satisfy minimal consumer demands.   *159*

PEOPLES DEMOCRACY: A term applied to the Communist-ruled states of Eastern Europe, suggesting that they are no longer capitalist countries but that they have likewise not achieved the degree of socialization now prevalent in the Soviet Union.

REVISIONISM: A concept, which dates back to the critique first made by the German socialist Eduard Bernstein, of Marxian economics and the Marxist prescription for revolution. In the mid-twentieth century the term refers to Communist leaders such as Joseph Tito who tend to reject the right of the Soviet Communist Party to dictate the policies of weaker Communist states and Parties. Contemporary revisionists also usually deny the inevitability of armed conflict between capitalist and Communist states and recognize, at least to a limited degree, the continued importance of nationalist sentiment even in Communist societies.

THAW: A word first employed in a political context by the Soviet writer Ilya Ehrenburg to denote the political relaxation, lessening of police terror and greater moderation on the part of Communist Party leadership which came about in the Soviet Union and the East European states in the wake of Stalin's death.

BOURGEOIS NATIONALISM: A term frequently used by Communists to characterize the behavior of their domestic opponents and individuals within their own ranks who decline to submit to rigid guidance by the Party and who are suspected of being unduly influenced by western concepts relating to arts and letters, material affluence and individual freedom.

DEMOCRATIC CENTRALISM: The principle that lower organs of a Communist Party must accept unequivocally the decisions of higher Party bodies. In effect it is this principle which has made all Communist Parties into hierarchies which are in practice ruled on a small oligarchy limited to Central Committee members.

POLYCENTRISM: A recent trend which has, in effect, ended the former monolithic unity of the World Communist Movement and the subservience of all Communist Parties to the Communist Party of the Soviet Union. Polycentrism may be seen as the cumulative result of Tito's break with Stalin in 1948, the subsequent emergence of National Communism in Hungary and Poland and, most recently, the ideological rift between Soviet and Chinese Communists. The term implies that individual Communist Parties now have greater freedom to formulate their own programs and that they are, consequently, no longer fully controlled from a single center of Communist power.

BIBLIOGRAPHY

Bain, Leslie B. *The Reluctant Satellites: An Eyewitness Report on East Europe and the Hungarian Revolution.* New York: Macmillan, 1960.

Balassa, M. *The Hungarian Experience in Economic Planning.* New Haven: Yale University Press, 1959.

Betts, R. R. (ed.). *Central and South-East Europe, 1945-1948.* London: Royal Institute of International Affairs, 1950.

Brzezinski, Z. K. *The Soviet Bloc.* New York: Praeger, 1961.

Dallin, Alexander (ed.). *The Anti-Stalin Campaign and International Communism.* New York: Columbia University Press, 1956.
────── (ed.). *Diversity in International Communism: A Documentary Record.* New York: Columbia University Press, 1963.

Dziewanowski, M. K. *The Communist Party of Poland.* Cambridge: Harvard University Press, 1959.

Fischer-Galati, Stephen (ed.). *Eastern Europe in the Sixties.* New York: Praeger, 1963.

Freidin, Seymour. *The Forgotten People.* New York: Charles Scribner's Sons, 1962.

Gibney, Frank. *The Frozen Revolution.* New York: Farrar, Straus & Cudahy, 1959.

Griffith, William E. *Albania and the Sino-Soviet Rift.* Cambridge: M.I.T. Press, 1963.

Hudson, G. F., *et.al. The Sino-Soviet Dispute.* New York: Praeger, 1961.

Kecskemeti, Paul. *The Unexpected Revolution: Social Forces in the Hungarian Uprising.* Stanford: Stanford University Press, 1961.

Kertesz, Stephen D. (ed.). *East Central Europe and the World.* Notre Dame: University of Notre Dame Press, 1962.
────── (ed.). *The Fate of East Central Europe.* Notre Dame: University of Notre Dame Press, 1956.

Korbel, Josef. *The Communist Subversion of Czechoslovakia, 1938-1948.* Princeton: Princeton University Press, 1959.

Lagovia, Donald S. *The Sino-Soviet Conflict, 1956-1961.* Princeton: Princeton University Press, 1962.

Laqueur, Walter, and Labedz, Leopold. *Polycentrism.* New York: Praeger, 1963.

Lasky, Melvin I. (ed.). *The Hungarian Revolution.* New York: Praeger, 1957.

Lewis, Flora. *A Case History of Hope.* New York: Doubleday, 1958.

Macartney, C. A., and Palmer, A. W. *Independent Eastern Europe.* New York: St Martin's Press, 1962.

Mevay, Tibor. *Thirteen Days That Shook The Kremlin.* New York: Praeger, 1959.

Milosz, Czeslaw. *The Captive Mind.* New York: Alfred A. Knopf, 1953.

Mosely, Philip E. (ed.). *The Kremlin and World Politics.* New York: Vintage, 1960.

Paloczi-Horvath, George. *The Undefeated.* Boston: Little, Brown, 1959.

Pryor, Frederick L. *The Communist Foreign Trade System.* Cambridge: M.I.T. Press, 1963.

Roberts, Henry L. *Rumania.* New Haven: Yale University Press, 1951.
——— (ed.). *The Satellites in Eastern Europe.* Vol. 317 of *The Annals of the American Academy of Political and Social Science.* Philadelphia, 1958.

Rothschild, Joseph. *The Communist Party of Bulgaria.* New York: Columbia University Press, 1959.

Seton-Watson, Hugh. *Eastern Europe Between the Wars, 1918-1941.* Cambridge: Cambridge University Press, 1946.
——— *The East European Revolution.* New York: Praeger, 1957.

Shepherd, Gordon. *Russia's Danubian Empire.* New York: Praeger, 1954.

Starr, Richard F. *Poland, 1944-1962: The Sovietization of a Captive People*. Baton Rouge: Louisiana University Press, 1962.

Stillman, Edmund O. (ed.). *Bitter Harvest: The Intellectual Revolt Behind the Iron Curtain*. New York: Praeger, 1959.

Taborsky, Edward. *Communism in Czechoslovakia, 1948-1960*. Princeton: Princeton University Press, 1961.

Vali, Ferenc A. *Rift and Revolt in Hungary*. Cambridge: Harvard University Press, 1961.

Wiskemann, Elizabeth. *Germany's Eastern Neighbors*. London: Oxford University Press, 1956.

Wolff, Robert Lee. *The Balkans in Our Time*. Cambridge: Harvard University Press, 1956.

Zinner, Paul E. *Communist Strategy and Tactics in Czechoslovakia, 1918-1948*. New York: Praeger, 1963.
———— *Revolution in Hungary*. New York: Columbia University Press, 1962.
———— (ed.). *National Communism and Popular Revolt in Eastern Europe*. New York: Columbia University Press, 1956.

Index

African students: Bulgaria, 57
Czechoslovakia, 33
Albania, 75-82
blockade, 81
Chinese Communists, 78-79
gift from, 81
Communist leaders, 75
Democratic Front, 75
Fourth Congress of Albanian
Communist Party, 81
Gheg clans, 77
People's Democratic Front, 75
resistance movements, 75-76
Soviet breaks off relationship, 81
Soviet Navy evacuates, 80
Third Congress of the Albanian
Communist Party, 78
Tito, 76-77, 81-82
Tosk people, 77
Anders, General Wladyslaw, 11n,
12

Barak, Rudolf, 30
Belishova, Liri, 80
Benes, Edward, 24, 26, 27
Berling, General Zygmunt, 12
Berman, Jakob, 18, 60
Bierut, Boleslaw, 60
Bodnaras, Emil, 44
Bulgaria, 48-57
African students, 57
economics, 55-57
Fatherland Front, 49, 50, 51, 52,
54
Fatherland Front Peasant
Union, 54
five-year plan, 57
peace treaty, 54
Peasant Union, 51-52, 54
Soviet, no reparations from, 50

Soviet declares war, 49
Tito cancels debt, 50
twenty-year plan, 57

Catholic Populist Party, 25-26
Chamberlain, Sir Austen, 2-3
Chamberlain, Neville, 2
Chervenkov, Valko, 55, 56
Chou En-lai, 81
Clementis, Vladimir, 29
Common Market, 74
Como, Maqo, 80
Council for Economic Mutual
Assistance, 47, 86-87
Crooked Circle of Warsaw, 59-60,
66
Cyrankiewicz, Josef, 18, 62
Czech (National) Socialist Party,
25
Czechoslovakia, 23-33
African students, 33
Catholic Populist Party, 25-26
Communist *coup*, 26, 27
constitution, new, 32
culture, 33
economics, 27-29, 31-32
elections of 1946, 25
five-year plan, third, 31
Lidice, 23
National Socialist Party, 25
Ruthenia, 24
Social Democrats, 26, 27

Damyanov, Georgi, 53
Dimitrov, Dr. G. M., 51, 52, 55

Eighth Congress of the
Communist Party, 73

Fatherland Front in Bulgaria,
49, 50, 51, 52, 54